Remembering Deir Yassin

The Future of Israel and Palestine

EDITED BY
Daniel A. McGowan and Marc H. Ellis

OLIVE
BRANCH
PRESS

An imprint of Interlink Publishing Group, Inc.
New York

First published in 1998 by

Olive Branch Press
An imprint of Interlink Publishing Group, Inc.
99 Seventh Avenue • Brooklyn, New York 11215

ISBN 1-56656-291-0

Printed and bound in Canada
10 9 8 7 6 5 4 3 2 1

Cover Painting Offered By Silent Auction

The front cover shows a beautiful oil painting by Ann Leggett of an original
Arab building that exists today at Deir Yassin. The figures are Arab and are
timeless. The piece is done with a seventeenth-century-style resin-oil medium.
It measures 10" by 12" and is being offered by silent auction with the final bid
to benefit "Deir Yassin Remembered" to be accepted on the 51st anniversary of
the Deir Yassin massacre on April 9, 1999. Please send bids to Daniel McGowan,
Deir Yassin Remembered, 4078 Scandling Center, Geneva, New York 14456 (USA).

Contents

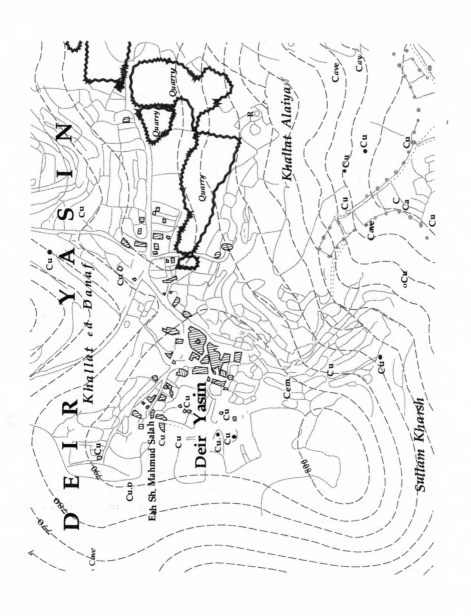

The Purpose of Deir Yassin Remembered

Deir Yassin Remembered is an organization of Jews and non-Jews working to build a memorial at Deir Yassin on the west side of Jerusalem within sight of Yad Vashem. It was here in April 1948 that a peaceful Palestinian Arab village was attacked and conquered. After the village fell under Jewish control more than a hundred Arabs were massacred. For Palestinians, this massacre has come to symbolize the destruction of Palestine.

Deir Yassin Remembered has grown out of the voice and vision of those, like Elie Wiesel, who extol the virtues of remembering and never forgetting the suffering of any people. It has also grown out of the realization by Palestinians that their tragic history in this century should be recognized more explicitly and more publicly than through traditional storytelling within families.

The struggle to build a memorial to those massacred at Deir Yassin 50 years ago is a struggle to change both Israeli and Palestinian thinking. It is a call to analyze and reject the myths that have been promulgated about Israeli and Palestinian history, including "a land without people" and "the purity of arms." And it is a call to end words without action and to contribute energy, time, and money to improve the welfare of the Palestinian people.

The goal of Deir Yassin Remembered is a simple one: the resurrection of this important piece of Palestinian history as a way to create a future where Israelis and Palestinians can live together in a just and equitable way. The international competition to design a memorial for the victims of Deir Yassin will be open to the international artistic community, including those in Israel. A prize of $50,000 or more will be offered to the winner of the competition. This competition, as well as other educational activities carried out by Deir Yassin Remembered will encourage education about the history of Deir Yassin and show how, one day, understanding of that tragedy may lead to justice and peace. Through international coverage and interest, Deir Yassin Remembered will encourage the government of Israel to provide a suitable site at Deir Yassin for this memorial. Of course, Israel may deny this proposal at first. But over time, more and more people around the world, including Jews, will come to understand that the denial of memorials to Palestinian suffering belittles their own memorials to their heroes of 1948 and even to the victims of other massacres, including those who died in the Holocaust. As an Israeli journalist recently wrote in *The Jerusalem Post*, "A memorial at Deir Yassin? How could we object?"

Deir Yassin Remembered has collected contributions from people all over the world. These have helped to defray the costs of our website www.deiryassin.org, our two international conferences, and one mission to the Israeli Knesset. We have received no help from any government, including the Palestinian Authority. The proceeds from the sale of this book will help us to continue the struggle.

Daniel A. McGowan
April 9, 1998

Preface

As Israel enters its sixth decade of existence, that nation's failings continue to have catastrophic effects for the Palestinian people. In reality the two are bound together, for the ingathering of Jews over the past 50 years has also meant the creation of a Palestinian diaspora. Though this diaspora, which exists within and outside of the state of Israel, is less often discussed than the drama of the creation of the Jewish state, its significance cannot be overstated. For the Palestinian people, the catastrophe which befell them is obvious in its importance, for it initiated a process of displacement, estrangement, and wandering which continues today. For Jews, this catastrophe is equally important, though not in such an obvious way. If Jewish self-worth and accomplishment is dependent on the catastrophe of the Palestinian people, then it becomes a void where the cries of the victims call out for an accounting.

The massacre of Palestinian Arabs at Deir Yassin in April 1948, an event which accompanied the creation of Israel, illustrates the connection between the histories of these two peoples in the past as it illuminates the connection today. Remembering the massacre, therefore, is as crucial today as it was in the past, perhaps even more so, for can there be a future of justice, peace, and harmony if the historical and contemporary dimensions of a shared history remain unacknowledged? Can there be a different history between Jews and Palestinians in the future if the past remains buried, as if the creation of the Jewish state was without victims?

At this crucial time in the history of Jews and Palestinians, when the hope of the past few years is diminishing, this volume attempts to pose a path beyond injustice, diaspora, and complicity. It does so by raising our consciousness about the massacre at Deir Yassin, for it is representative of the Palestinian catastrophe and is a way of remembering the past. As a number of authors in this volume point out, the memorial to the Jewish dead of the Holocaust is within eyesight of the massacre site at Deir Yassin. Deir Yassin, once a Palestinian village, and now with a Jewish population within the borders of Israel, lacks a memorial of any kind. Could the memorialization of the Palestinian catastrophe at Deir Yassin be a place of pilgrimage for Palestinians and Jews, as Yad Vashem has become such a place for Jews and non-

Jews concerned for justice around the world? Could Deir Yassin and Yad Vashem become gathering places for Palestinians and Jews who acknowledge the past and commit themselves to a future of justice and reconciliation?

The first half of this book focuses on the Palestinian catastrophe through the lens of Deir Yassin, and concludes with a proposed design for such a memorialization; the second half of the book deals with how such a memory might lead to a future where Jews and Palestinians affirm each other and acknowledge their equal rights throughout the land. Here we have authors approaching the future from a variety of perspectives, though with a common objective: using memory as a path to the future. (In fact, the variety of perspectives even shape some of the statistical memory: figures for the number of people killed at Deir Yassin have most often settled at 254, but some of the contributors relied on reports indicating lower figures and we have chosen to leave each contributor's judgment intact.)

Remembering for the future. Such a memorable phrase has been used as a theme for Holocaust remembrance and applies here as well. The memory of the Holocaust, of course, is not just for Jews but also is for the perpetrators as well as for those who remained silent. So, too, the catastrophe of the Palestinians is a memory for those who suffer and those who caused that suffering. Deir Yassin is therefore for both Palestinians and Jews. But, as with the Holocaust, the memory of Deir Yassin can become in the future a memory that moves beyond victim and victor and thus is universal in its importance. "Never again" is a phrase which resounds in the history of the Jewish people and throughout the world. In its application to the Palestinian people, the phrase achieves even more depth and universality. At the same time, if Jews and Palestinians meet in the brokenness of their respective histories — at memorials at Deir Yassin and at Yad Vashem — then a healing of their histories might emerge while providing a model to the world for ending the cycle of violence. Remembering for the future becomes a path of activity with revolutionary implications for Jewish and Palestinian history and beyond.

For many, the accounts of the atrocity at Deir Yassin, recounted here by Palestinians and a Jewish Israeli, will be difficult to read both because of the sheer horror of these deaths and because the narrative of Jewish innocence is quite strong in the West, especially after the Holocaust. The recognition explored in other essays that this massacre was hardly unique and that the creation of Israel was dependent on the cleansing of hundreds of thousands of Arabs from Palestine may be even more difficult to accept. Nonetheless, the reality remains and the inclusion of Palestinian suffering into the narrative of Jews in Israel and the West is essential if the truth is to be faced. Deir Yassin is not the only face of Israel and the Jewish people; still it is part of the story of post-Holocaust Jewish life which must be written about and admitted. As Souad Dajani makes clear in her essay, the attempt to cover up the truth does not replace the truth. Only by taking a stand rooted in the truths which she and other Palestinians experience can the politics of injustice be reversed. Remembering Deir Yassin may point toward a future solution that is a more far-reaching and satisfying sharing of Israel/Palestine than earlier proposals for a two-state settlement. Mohammed Hallaj names this as the possibility of Arab-Jewish humanism.

What would this Arab-Jewish humanism look like in practice? This book only suggests its possibility. The memory of suffering can be used in two ways: as a blunt instrument to achieve power or as a path of solidarity with others who are suffering. In these pages this latter path is only hinted at because the former has so often triumphed in the history of the state of Israel. The memory of suffering as a path of solidarity is found here, too, though diminished and weak. Could suffering as solidarity be raised to a new level of speech and activity in recognizing the wrong which has been committed and memorializing the dead of Deir Yassin?

In proposing such a memorial and writing this book the editors and contributors seek this vision of a future that remembers suffering as a way of creating a land and world where suffering is a memory that becomes so distant that the need for new memorials is mitigated or even ended. The time for solidarity with the dead as a form of solidarity with the living is now in a land that many call holy. Yet to begin that journey is to face the most difficult of truths about history, even about one's own people.

Part One

Remembering Deir Yassin

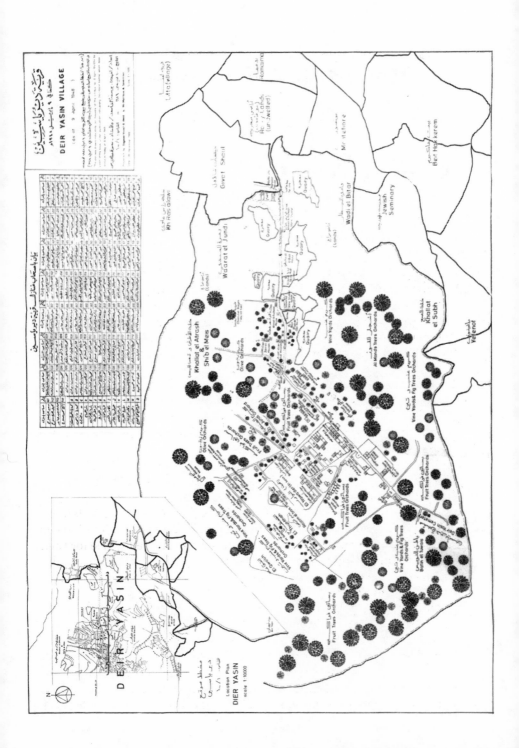

DEIR YASIN VILLAGE

Location Plan
DIER YASIN
scale 1:10000

DEIR YASIN

1

Deir Yassin Remembered

by Daniel McGowan

Early in the morning of Friday, April 9, 1948, 130 commandos of the Irgun and the Stern Gang attacked Deir Yassin, a village with about 750 Palestinian residents. It was several weeks before the end of British Mandate rule in Palestine. The village lay outside of the area assigned by the United Nations to the Jewish State; it had a peaceful reputation. But it was located on high ground in the corridor between Tel Aviv and Jerusalem. By the end of the day, over 100 Palestinians, children, women, and men, were dead. It was a massacre, and the participants knew it. The leaders of the mainstream Zionist army, the Haganah, had distanced themselves from their peripheral participation in the attack and issued a statement denouncing the dissidents of Irgun and the Stern Gang just as they had after the attack on the King David Hotel in July 1946. They admitted that the massacre "disgraced the cause of Jewish fighters and dishonored Jewish arms and the Jewish flag." They played down the fact that their Palmach troops had reinforced the terrorist attack, even though they did not participate in the massacre and looting subsequent to it.

David Ben-Gurion even sent an apology to King Abdullah, leader of TransJordan. But according to Menachem Begin, the leader of the Irgun at the time (although he was not at Deir Yassin), this horrific act served the future state of Israel well. In his book *The Revolt*, Begin claimed: "Arabs throughout the country, induced to believe wild tales of 'Irgun butchery,' were seized with limitless panic and started to flee for their lives. This mass flight soon developed into a maddened, uncontrollable stampede. The political and economic significance of this development can hardly be overestimated."

Of about 144 houses at Deir Yassin only a few were destroyed. By September, Orthodox Jewish immigrants from Poland, Romania, and Slovakia settled there over the objections of Martin Buber, Cecil Roth, and others, who believed that the site of the massacre should be left uninhabited. The center of the village was renamed Kfar Shaul. The cemetery was bulldozed, and like hundreds of other Palestinian villages to follow, Deir Yassin was wiped off the map. As Jerusalem expanded, the lands of Deir Yassin became a part of the city and it is now known simply as the area between Givat Shaul and the settlement of Har Nof.

Why We Remember Deir Yassin

The primary purpose of Deir Yassin Remembered is to build a memorial at Deir Yassin to the Palestinian victims who were massacred there on April 9, 1948. We define "massacre" in the words of Colin Edwards as "the deliberate killing of captive civilians." There is no doubt that what occurred at Deir Yassin was not a battle; it was unequivocally a massacre. And this single event is one of the most significant in twentieth century Palestinian and Israeli history, not because of its size or its brutality, but because it marked the beginning of the depopulation of over 400 Arab villages and cities and the expulsion of over 700,000 Palestinian inhabitants to make room for victims of the Holocaust and other Jews from the rest of the world. The story of Deir Yassin is a story of two peoples' struggle for the same land. The details of that story are important for both the victor and the victim.

Although most scholars no longer believe that Israel was "a land without people for a people without land," many others believe the myth today. Resurrecting the memory of Deir Yassin serves to dispel this propaganda. Palestinians were dispossessed in 1948 and continue to be dispossessed today in the name of building an expanding Jewish state.

If Jewish rights to property seized during the Holocaust in Europe are valid (and I believe they are), why are claims to restitution of Palestinian property in Deir Yassin and all the other cities and villages not valid? After the massacre at Deir Yassin the Haganah promised, "We will maintain the graves and the remaining property and return it to the owners when the time comes." Is it not appropriate to ask when that time will come?

Our call to remember the significance of Deir Yassin, our use of the motto of the Simon Wiesenthal Center, "Hope lives when people remember," and our use of the sabra cactus as a logo have caused some to condemn this project. The heart of such objections is that "remembering" a catastrophe such as occurred at Deir Yassin (and the ethnic cleansing which it precipitated) is reminiscent of the Holocaust, and we are taught there was only one Holocaust and that refers to the persecution of Jews by the Nazis. Palestinians are simply not allowed to acknowledge their holocaust. Theirs was a "depopulation," a "making room" for truly persecuted people who were returning to land from which they were driven 2,000 years ago.

Likewise "Islamic" or "Arab terrorism" is taken for granted; the term "Jewish terrorism" borders on or anti-Semitism and must be disguised or denied or ignored as much as possible. By any definition, Deir Yassin was unequivocally a terrorist attack. But since it was in the context of "building a Jewish State," it is deliberately ignored in the West. With overwhelming evidence of the atrocities committed, as well as the condemnation by Jewish leaders from Ben-Gurion to Buber to Albert Einstein, denial is impossible. The alternative is silence. Deir Yassin Remembered challenges that silence.

Many students interviewed at Hebrew University have not even heard of Deir Yassin or the destruction of Palestinian villages in general. Most have visited Israel's Holocaust memorial, Yad Vashem, never realizing that it looks across at Deir Yassin about 1,500 yards to the north. In his essay, "Zionism as a Test Case in the Morality of Nationalism," Elias Baumgarten concludes by saying:

> Acknowledging the violation of Palestinian rights is a prerequisite of a morally acceptable Jewish nationalism. The duty to acknowledge and make restitution also suggests the kind of practical measures Israel should take in the current conflict... It should teach in its schools the truth about the destruction of Arab villages in Israel... It should create memorials and commemorative holidays for Palestinian victims. Israel should, in short, create a Jewish nationalism with a transformed relationship both to its own past and, in the present, to the Palestinian people.

Deir Yassin Remembered is an organization of Jews and non-Jews with a mission to do exactly that.

Board of Advisers

From the outset the board was deliberately structured to include half Jews, half non-Jews, half men and half women. This was not just an attempt to be politically correct. Rather, it is based on the belief that to remember Deir Yassin is important for both the victor and the victim and both should take part in it.

At present our board of advisers consists of 20 people. The board represents a remarkable collection of leaders with one common thread, namely a strong conviction that the memory of Deir Yassin should not be forgotten. For such a small number of people, the diversity is astounding. Some are very rich; some are very poor. There are Muslims, Jews, Christians, and agnostics. There are politicians turned academics and academics turned politicians. There are those with tenure and security and others whose involvement with the project could cost them their jobs and endanger their families.

Some are most interested in building and documenting the

Palestinian history; others work toward a new theology which tries to answer the questions people must ask about history they are now creating; in strength (and, indeed, to preserve strength) they want to restore the tradition of critical thinking demonstrated by Walter Benjamin, Hannah Arendt, and Martin Buber. They want to restore the moral vision of the Jewish people seeking justice for all; they want to open the doors of those who systematically ignore injustices against the Palestinians.

Revelations: Yad Vashem

Most Israelis and most visitors to Israel do not go to Deir Yassin. Tour guides in Jerusalem are mostly Jewish and, the location of Deir Yassin and the true story of the massacre is not on their agenda. So it is startling to realize that much of the actual village of Deir Yassin remains largely intact in the form of a mental hospital in the Givat Shaul district of West Jerusalem. The remaining Palestinian buildings are beautiful and quite distinctive in style and color from other buildings in the area. They are surrounded by the Orthodox Jewish settlement of Har Nof and the industrial area of Givat Shaul. There are no markers, no plaques, and no memorials at Deir Yassin; parking is a problem and access to the mental hospital grounds is, understandably, restricted.

Most visitors and virtually all politicians visit the most famous Holocaust museum. Yad Vashem means literally "a monument and a name" (or figuratively "a monument and a memorial") and comes from Isaiah, where God says to those who keep his covenant, "I will give them... a monument and a name... I will give them an everlasting name that shall never be effaced." Conceived in 1942 and codified in the 1953 Law of Remembrance of Shoah and Heroism — Yad Vashem, this memorial park is Israel's preeminent national shrine.

One of the most important tasks of Yad Vashem has been to record the names of every Jewish victim of the Germans to perpetuate the memory of the martyrs whose graves are unknown and unmarked. As James Young says in his book *The Texture of Memory*, "The function of memory in this project is precisely what it has always been for the Jewish nation; in addition to bringing home the 'national lessons' of the Holocaust, memory would work to bind present and past generations, to unify a world outlook, to create a vicariously shared national experience."

Of course, this is exactly the underlying task of Deir Yassin Remembered in its quest to build a memorial at Deir Yassin. For Palestinians, the memory of Deir Yassin is paramount and cannot be denied. To paraphrase Young, the function of memory in this project is precisely what it has always been for the Palestinian nation; in addition to bringing home the 'national lessons' of the Catastrophe of 1948, memory works to bind present and past generations, to unify a world outlook, to create a vicariously shared national experience.

Chilling is the fact that the Deir Yassin massacre took place within sight of the national memorial at Yad Vashem. Only a mile from where Jewish martyrs are memorialized lie the Palestinian martyrs of Deir Yassin whose graves are unknown and unmarked. The irony is breathtaking. While the idea of Yad Vashem was conceived long before the massacre, construction began years after it. Were the ghosts of Deir Yassin ignored or simply bulldozed over? In dedication ceremonies at Yad Vashem, did anyone ever look to the north and remember Deir Yassin? Did anyone speak of it; or were its martyrs so deeply buried that their cries for justice went unheard?

Tours

Palestinians, Israelis, and a few foreign visitors are beginning to take limited tours of some of the Arab villages depopulated in 1948. To the best of my knowledge, only the Alternative Information Center and the Middle East Council of Churches include Deir Yassin in tours of Jerusalem. From a different perspective, there are special tours led by surviving underground fighters or "battle participants" such as Ezra Yachin and Yehuda Lapidot. The latest of these (led by Lapidot) was sponsored by the Society for the Protection of Nature in Israel (SPNI) and by ETZEL Veterans League (survivors of the Irgun); it usually occurs every April 9th on the anniversary of the "battle" and celebrates it from the radical Zionist point of view. These tours deny there was a massacre and they greatly inflate the number of Jewish casualties. No mention is made of the male prisoners who were paraded through the Zakhron Yosef quarter in Jerusalem before being taken to the stone quarry between Deir Yassin and Givat Shaul where, in the words of an eyewitness, they were "put against the wall and shot to death."

When ordinary tourists ask about Deir Yassin they usually receive the following response. On a typical tour, the guide will simply (and often truthfully) deny ever having heard of it. It is not on any tourist maps. (That was not always the case; on pre-1948 maps Deir Yassin is clearly shown and is likely to have been visited by religious tours of old monasteries. The word "deir" (or "dir" or "dayr") means monastery, and there was a large ruin at the southwestern edge of the village which was simply known as the "Deir.")

Memories

It was Martin Buber who wrote to Ben-Gurion saying, "In Deir Yassin hundreds of innocent men, women, and children were massacred. The Deir Yassin affair is a black stain on the honor of the Jewish nation. The Zionist movement, the army, and our government of the time (the Jewish Agency Executive), all felt this acutely and most unequivocally condemned the deed." It was Albert Einstein (and other Jewish leaders) who publicly expressed shock and outrage over the massacre and the pride shown by the Irgunists and the Sternists when they "publicized it widely, and invited all the foreign correspondents present in the country to view the heaped corpses and the general havoc at Deir Yassin." The two gangs were accused of inaugurating "a reign of terror in the Palestine Jewish community. Teachers were beaten up for speaking against them, adults were shot for not letting their children join them. By gangster methods, beatings, window-smashing and widespread robberies, the terrorists intimidated the population and exacted a heavy tribute."

In his book, *Jewish History, Jewish Religion*, Israel Shahak, a Holocaust survivor and life-long human rights activist writes

> But we can derive from this analysis another, more general conclusion about the most effective and horrific means of compulsion to do evil, to cheat and to deceive and, while keeping one's hands quite clean of violence, to corrupt whole peoples and drive them to oppression and murder. (For there can no longer be any doubt that the most horrifying acts of oppression in the West Bank are motivated by Jewish religious fanaticism.)... Unlike Stalin's tame scholars, the rabbis — and even more so the scholars attacked here, and with them the whole mob of equally silent middlebrows such as writers, journalists, public figures, who lie and deceive more than they — are not facing the danger of death or concentration camp, but only social pressure; they lie out of patriotism because they believe that it is their duty to lie for what they conceive to be the Jewish interest. They are patriotic liars, and it is the same patriotism which reduces them to silence when confronted with the discrimination and oppression of the Palestinians.

To paraphrase Nachum Goldman, former president of the World Jewish Congress, the State of Israel came into being not only by virtue of the blood spilt by those who fell in battles for its existence, but also, indirectly, because of those murdered in the Holocaust. Those martyrs are honored at Yad Vashem and at many other Holocaust memorials all over the world.

Likewise the State of Palestine will come into being not only by the blood of those fighting for the rights and for the identity of the Palestinian people, but also, indirectly, because of those murdered at (and with the memory of) Deir Yassin.

Remember Deir Yassin! has been a slogan of propaganda and it has been a battle cry. It is time now for it to be turned around. It is time for the real memory of Deir Yassin to be the medium for mutual recognition of two people living on the same land. It is time for Palestinians to visit Yad Vashem and to create their own memorials to bind present and past generations, to unify a world outlook, and to create a vicariously shared national experience. And it is time for Israelis to remember and actually visit Deir Yassin. Reconstructing memory is clearly a task for both peoples.

2

Remembering Deir Yassin: A Reflection on Memory and Justice

by Marc H. Ellis

In the summer of 1995 the Israeli-Palestinian negotiations reached another milestone with further Israeli withdrawal from occupied Palestinian territory and the expanded assumption of governance by the Palestinian National Authority. It was at this time that I received an invitation to join the Board of Advisers of a project entitled "Deir Yassin Remembered." The project, had as its purpose the creation of a memorial site to commemorate the massacre of more than 100 Palestinian Arabs at Deir Yassin by Jewish soldiers in April 1948. Among the perpetrators of the massacre was the Irgun, a radical military arm in the struggle for the establishment of a Jewish state, whose leader, Menachem Begin, would later become prime minister of Israel.

Though by the spring of 1948 both sides of the Jewish-Arab conflict in Palestine were growing accustomed to the human cost of war, this massacre provoked an outrage which to this day remains a sensitive part of the history of both peoples. Located strategically on high ground in the corridor between Tel Aviv and Jerusalem, Deir Yassin had a peaceful reputation among its neighboring Jewish settlements and had entered into a mutual non-aggression pact with the Givat-Shaul and Montefiore settlements. When Arab forces asked permission to use Deir Yassin as a military base, the village leaders refused, pleading that its strategic location would expose the village, especially its women and children, to great danger. Deir Yassin's leaders foresaw the possibility which then arrived despite their delicate and seemingly successful negotiations with the Jewish villages and Arab combatants, for Deir Yassin was captured after an unsuccessful defense against the Irgun and Stern Gang, as well as the Haganah, the mainstream Jewish army. After the Haganah withdrew its men, the Irgun and Stern Gang remained. Looting, maiming, and murder followed the surrender of the village. The message that Begin and the Irgun successfully conveyed to the

Palestinian Arabs was that they must flee the advancing Jewish armies or face dire consequences. Within weeks of the massacre hundreds of thousands of Arabs fled their homes. As Begin noted in his memoirs, the "legend" of Deir Yassin was "worth half a dozen battalions to the forces of Israel." After the massacre, Begin sent a message of congratulations to the conquerors of Deir Yassin: "Accept congratulations on this splendid act of conquest. Tell the soldiers you have made history in Israel."

After initially claiming that a group of Arab rebels was responsible for the massacre, the Jewish Agency acknowledged that Jewish soldiers belonging to dissident organizations were responsible for the "savage and barbaric" acts at Deir Yassin and cabled an apology to King Abdullah, the leader of TransJordan. A year later, as plans for resettlement of the abandoned village by Jewish Israelis were being formulated, Martin Buber and three other Jewish scholars — Ernst Simon, Werner Senator, and Cecil Roth — wrote to Prime Minister David Ben-Gurion asking that Deir Yassin be left uninhabited, or at least that its resettlement be postponed. Noting the tremendous pressures of resettlement resulting from the displacement of Jewish populations during World War II, the authors still pleaded for a higher consideration. For Deir Yassin had become "infamous throughout the Jewish world, the Arab world and the whole world. In Deir Yassin hundreds of innocent men, women, and children were massacred. The Deir Yassin affair is a black stain on the honor of the Jewish nation." The letter continued:

> it would be better to let the lands of Deir Yassin lie fallow and the houses of Deir Yassin stand uninhabited, than to carry out an act whose negative symbolic impact is infinitely greater than the practical resolution it can offer. Resettling Deir Yassin within a year of the crime, and without the framework of ordinary settlement, would amount to an endorsement of, or at least an acquiescence with, the massacre. Let the village of Deir Yassin remain uninhabited for the time being, and let its desolation be a terrible and tragic symbol of war, and a warning to our people that no practical or military needs may ever justify such acts of murder and that the nation does not wish to profit from them.

Ben-Gurion did not respond to the letter, despite the fact that Buber and his compatriots sent him copy after copy, anticipating a response. Eventually the prime minister's secretary responded that Ben-Gurion was simply too busy to read their letters. Meanwhile the plans for resettlement continued unabated. Indeed, the press reported the resettlement of the village, with the new name of Givat Shaul Bet, as if it were like any other. The Israeli historian Tom Segev writes that, "Several hundred guests came to the opening ceremony, including

Cabinet Ministers Kaplan and Shapira, as well as the Chief Rabbis and the Mayor of Jerusalem. President Haim Weizmann sent written congratulations. The band of the school for the blind played and refreshments were served."

When I received my invitation to join the Deir Yassin commemoration committee, I thought of this history of atrocity, the letter of conscience, and the silence of Ben-Gurion. Surely Ben-Gurion was a busy man, as the creation of a state takes an extraordinary amount of energy, ingenuity, political maneuvering, and vision. The deed done, a thousand issues confronting him in the present, who would not excuse him this oversight, or even refusal, to reply? The celebration is also understandable, for is not the creation of a new community a cause for festivities rather than confessions of misdeeds, even atrocity?

From another perspective, Ben-Gurion's silence signaled a question which to this day has yet to be answered. According to the Israeli historian Benny Morris, it was during the time of the massacre at Deir Yassin that Ben-Gurion "explicitly sanctioned the expulsion of Arabs from a whole area of Palestine." Was Ben-Gurion's silence an attempt to dismiss or even bury the reality that the founding of the state of Israel was marked by atrocity and violence rather than innocence, and that many survivors of the Holocaust achieved security and prosperity with the spoils of war and the displacement of another people? The Israeli newspaper *Davar* reported this haunting possibility without ambivalence: "At the sound of the Israeli soldiers marching, the Arabs were seized with a great terror and left their homes, with their heavily-loaded camels and donkeys, en route for the border... And now in Jamsin — renamed Givat Amal — live new residents, recently arrived via Cyprus, survivors of the camps of Europe. They sit around a long table, with one remnant of the abandoned furniture, and tell their tales." At the time of the resettlement of Deir Yassin, and hundreds of other formerly Arab villages, a Knesset member, Yosef Lamm, stated, "None of us behaved during the war in a way we might have expected the Jewish people to behave, either with regard to property or human life, and we should all be ashamed."

If the building of a state and the emergency circumstances of the Holocaust can account for the silence of Ben-Gurion — indeed the silence of much of the Jewish establishment inside and outside of Israel since Deir Yassin — what accounts for the silence today? Should letters like Buber's, updated and expanded over the years for other displacements and atrocities, remain unanswered? Should festivities that surrounded the signing of the 1993 Israel-PLO Declaration of Principles in Washington, D.C. be the order of the day, rather than remembrance of the cries accompanying the ending of Palestinian life and the beginning of new life for Jews in Israel? In short, should Deir Yassin, buried in Jewish consciousness, be raised again at this new and more promising moment in history? Or do remembrances of past transgressions freeze us — Jews and Palestinians — in a past from which there is no escape?

It is interesting that this argument is often promoted by parts of the Jewish establishment, even as they mobilize funds to create memorials such as the United States Holocaust Memorial Museum. We as Jews will not allow the world to forget our suffering at the hands of the Nazis and choose, within the context of unparalleled security and affluence in America, to emphasize the Holocaust as an essential element of Jewish identity. Does the emphasis on our suffering in Europe stifle a promising future in America and in Jewish communities around the world? Elie Wiesel's words at the fiftieth anniversary commemoration of the liberation of Auschwitz speak eloquently to this point: "Close your eyes and listen to the silent screams that terrify mothers. Listen to the prayers of anguished old men and women. Listen to the tears of the children. Remember the nocturnal procession of children, of more and more children, so frightened, so quiet, so beautiful. If we could simply look at one, our hearts would break. But it did not break the hearts of the murderers. Do not forgive the murderers and their accomplices. God, merciful God, do not have mercy on those who had no mercy on Jewish children." Wiesel spoke these words as a survivor of Auschwitz but also as an author, respected university professor, and Nobel Prize recipient.

One wonders if this very remembering, so detailed and yet at the same time so liturgically rendered, is the very key to remembering the suffering of those at Deir Yassin. The context and the magnitude of suffering were vastly different. There is no need to compare the tragedies to recognize that the tears of the children, the silent screams that terrify mothers, the prayers of anguished old men, resound in the history of the Palestinian people — in their catastrophe — just as they are heard in contemporary Jewish life. For if the Holocaust represents a tragic end to Jewish exile and powerlessness, the creation of the state of Israel represents the beginning of Palestinian exile and powerlessness. While the tragedies of the Holocaust and the Palestinian exile are separate in geography and magnitude, what connects them is a cycle of displacement that compounds and deepens the tragedy. That many Jews do not recognize this cycle carries the wounds of both peoples into the present and, in a sense, makes them more difficult to heal. For can Jews be healed of the trauma of Holocaust by displacing another people? Could it be that atrocities committed against the Palestinian people in Deir Yassin, and the inability to admit and confess this atrocity, have further wounded the Jewish people and made it more difficult for Jews, even with the power of Israel, to be healed? Wiesel's words, while so moving and powerful, mean less when he, like Ben-Gurion before him, responds to an invitation to remember Deir Yassin

— to be part of the Board of Advisers — with silence, and a brief mention that, with the peace process, "things are improving." Do Jews minimize the Holocaust because "things are improving" for Jews? Or does the naming of the historical injury deepen precisely at this moment?

Haunting Memories/Dreams of Innocence

Perhaps Wiesel is so immersed in commemorating the Jewish dead and celebrating Israel that he is unable to remember the cries of others whose lives and deaths are remembered by their own families with as much affection and horror as Wiesel has for his own. Perhaps at a deeper level, Wiesel is traumatized by the Holocaust and unable to think through the ambivalent feelings he might have toward both Israel and the Palestinians. Could Wiesel in his own anguish listen to a Palestinian man of his own age, whose parents and siblings were murdered at Deir Yassin, recite at the fiftieth anniversary of the massacre, "Do not forgive the murderers and their accomplices. God, merciful God, do not have mercy on those who had no mercy on Palestinian children"?

As Buber's letter to Ben-Gurion illustrates, not all Jews were too busy or silent in the face of Deir Yassin. In fact there were Jews who attempted to stop the massacre. Meir Pa'il, a young Haganah officer was present during the attack on Deir Yassin. According to Pa'il, when members of the neighboring Jewish village of Givat Shaul heard about the massacre, they came to Deir Yassin to stop the killing. As Pa'il relates: "They were just Jews, citizens who were ashamed. They began to shout and cry and the massacre was stopped." Unfortunately, despite the intervention of the Jewish villagers, the terror continued a few days longer. Some of the Arab survivors of Deir Yassin were loaded into freight trucks and "led in a victory parade like a Roman triumph" through the Mahaneh Yehuda and Zichron Yosef quarters of Jerusalem. After the parade, they were executed. Jacques de Reynier, a Swiss doctor working for the International Red Cross, arrived at the village as "mopping up" operations were being conducted. De Reynier witnessed, among other acts, a young Jewish woman stab an elderly man and woman "cowering on the doorsteps of their hut," and "a beautiful young girl with criminal eyes showed me her knife still dripping with blood, she displayed it like a trophy."

The horror of Deir Yassin continued to haunt Martin Buber. In an address to the American Friends of Ichud in New York in 1958, Buber recalled the breakdown of moral fiber witnessed a decade earlier: "It happened one day, however, that outside of all regular conduct of the war, a band of armed Jews fell on an Arab village and destroyed it. Often in earlier times Arab hordes had committed outrages of this kind and my soul bled with the sacrifice; but here it was a matter of our own, or my own crime, of the crime of Jews against the spirit. Even today I cannot think about this without feeling myself guilty." In this speech Buber accepted the verdict of history — that a Jewish state had come into being — and that contemporary Jewish life would be worked out within that structure. Still Buber felt that those Jews "who will truly serve the spirit must seek to make good all that was once missed: [they] must seek to free once against the blocked path to an understanding with the Arab peoples... There can be no peace between Jews and Arabs that is only a cessation of war; there can only be a peace of genuine cooperation." These comments harkened back to his letter to Ben-Gurion in which he wrote: "The time will come when it will be possible to conceive of some act in Deir Yassin, an act which will symbolize our people's desire for justice and brotherhood with the Arab people."

The distance between Buber and Wiesel on this issue is worth noting, for it illustrates how far the Jewish community has moved over the years. The distance cannot be explained simply by the origins or experience of either man, for both were formed in the crucible of the Nazi onslaught, and in their survival both were celebrated persons within and outside of the Jewish community. To understand their differences does not require us to romanticize Buber, as he was a man of his time, European in outlook, colonial in mentality, Zionist in his vision. But he was also able to deal with the issues of the Holocaust, Israel and the Palestinian Arabs in a critical and humane manner. In 1953, for example, Buber traveled from Jerusalem to accept the Peace Prize of the German Book Trade at Frankfurt and, in a controversial speech, differentiated between those Germans who committed genocide against the Jewish people, those who remained silent during the Nazi era, and those who actively resisted fascism. In Buber's view, he had only "in a formal sense a common humanity" with the perpetrators; knowing the "weakness of men" he could not condemn those who were unwilling to oppose the Nazis at risk of their own or their families' lives. However, for those who became martyrs, Buber felt a "reverence and a love, a special intimacy which binds us at times to the dead and to them alone." On the question of Palestine, Buber was a confirmed and outspoken proponent of a binational state, a land of two peoples jointly governed with a shared civic, defense, police, and economic system. After the establishment of the state of Israel, Buber argued for a federation within the Middle East and a healing of wounds within historic Palestine.

Two examples beyond the letter to Ben-Gurion regarding Deir Yassin illustrate Buber's direct confrontation of Israeli state power with regard to Palestinian Arabs: a March 1949 debate on the moral character of Israel with David Ben-Gurion just after the latter was installed as the first elected prime minister of the new state, in which Buber spoke of the Arab refugees as a moral question for Israel; and a March 1953 letter to the speaker of the Knesset protesting the draft legislation entitled "Expropriation of the Land," which legalized mass expropriation of Arab land within Israel. In the debate with Ben-Gurion, Buber challenged the new prime minister to convene an international, interfaith congress with the cooperation of Jews and the "neighboring peoples" to consider the refugee problem, adding the poignant question, "Were we not refugees in the diaspora?" In his protest against expropriation of Arab lands, Buber wrote, "We fail to understand why, according to press reports, hardly a single Jewish member of the Knesset has raised his voice against a law intended to give the stamp of legality to acts and deeds which he would consider a grave injustice if they were directed against himself or against Jewish property."

Nor do we need or want to demonize Wiesel in this comparison. Buber was expelled from Nazi Germany; Wiesel survived Auschwitz as an orphan, having lost his immediate family there. After his expulsion, Buber lived in Palestine and then Israel, and so was more closely attuned to the realities and the possibilities of the conflict between Jew and Arab. After two years in Palestine and Israel, Wiesel made his home in France and the United States and thus observed Israel from a distance. Perhaps because of the immediacy of the situation, for Buber the Holocaust becomes the backdrop for the establishment of a Jewish home in Palestine in cooperation with the Palestinian Arabs. In a February 1939 letter to Mohandas K. Gandhi, Buber condemned Gandhi's insistence on non-violence for German Jews, and disputed Gandhi's characterization of Jewish settlement in Palestine as a purely colonial endeavor, while still arguing for Jew and Arab to share Palestine. For Buber, Gandhi misunderstood both the absolute and unstoppable evil of the Nazi menace and the Jewish sense of peoplehood. Even within the dynamic of fascism and conflicting interests in Palestine, though, reconciliation and cooperation were possible. Hence Buber's travel and public lectures in Germany in the 1950s, at a time when Wiesel was observing his ten-year vow of silence on the Holocaust. When finally in the 1960s and 70s Wiesel spoke and wrote on the question of Jews and Palestinians, he did so within the context of the Holocaust, projecting the past into the present. That is why Wiesel flew to Israel on the second day of the 1967 war, expecting Israel's defeat and a second holocaust. Because of this expectation, the victory of Israel became a miracle, assured not by military strategy and tactics, but by the "millions of martyrs of the Holocaust [who] were enlisted in the ranks." For Wiesel, these martyrs were like the biblical pillars of fire shielding their spiritual heirs. With this assistance, Israel could not be defeated, and the Israeli victory became a watershed experience for Wiesel and the Jewish people.

For Wiesel, Israel represents a moral victory illustrated by the fact that during the war Israeli soldiers, rather than becoming cruel, became "sad"; in his view they fought without hate and, instead of becoming prideful, were humble and humane in their victories. Clearly, though Buber thought Jews to be superior to Arabs, he did not accord his own people this posture of innocence and, as with Deir Yassin, was direct and uncompromising concerning Jewish transgressions. For Buber, Jewish ethics were being sorely tried in Palestine/Israel, and the justification for Jewish renewal on the land was not innocence, but a responsibility to a future for both Jew and Arab. Both Buber and Wiesel correctly believed in Jewish innocence regarding the Holocaust. But Buber understood that the creation of a Jewish home, though absolutely essential, was not innocent in its reality, while Wiesel projects into the messy business of state building the innocence of the suffering.

This sense of Jewish innocence allows Wiesel to project a culpability on Palestinians which, from the Palestinian perspective, and especially in light of Deir Yassin, should rightfully be applied to Jews. In a letter "To a Young Palestinian Arab," published in 1975, Wiesel relates how Jews after the Holocaust "opted for Man" instead of vengeance. The pursuit of Nazi war criminals, for example, was to "remind man of his need to be human — not of his right to punish. On behalf of the dead we sought consolation, not retribution." In terms of Palestinians, Wiesel affirms, in a general way, responsibility for what happened to them; still he cannot accept what Palestinians have done with their anger:

> From Munich to Maalot, from Lod to Entebbe, from hijacking to hijacking, from ambush to ambush, you have spread terror among unarmed civilians and thrown into mourning families already too often visited by death. You will tell me that all these acts have been the work of your extremist comrades, not yours; but they acted on your behalf, with your approval, since you did not raise your voice to reason with them. You will tell me that it is your tragedy which incited them to murder. By murdering, they de based that tragedy, they betrayed it. Suffering is often unjust, but it never justifies murder.

It is this sense of innocence, rather than a commitment to Israel, that allows Wiesel to write these words without understanding that to an outside observer they are immediately relevant to contemporary Jewish history. For in light of Deir Yassin, it is untrue to say that Jews opted only for man, or that Jews did not seek vengeance. Can we see in this massacre that the Jews who maimed and killed — remembering that the leader of the Irgun, Menachem Begin, later became prime minister — in Wiesel's words "debased that tragedy, they betrayed it?" As Wiesel writes, "Suffering is often unjust, but it never justifies murder." Perhaps this is the subtext of Arthur Hertzberg's open letter to Elie Wiesel in August 1988, at the height of the Palestinian intifada, criticizing Wiesel's silence on the Israeli occupation and his refusal to publicly criticize Israeli policies. Hertzberg ends his letter with words reminiscent of Martin Buber: "We show the truest love of Israel and the Jewish people when we remind ourselves that, in strength or in weakness, we survive not by prudence and not by power, but through justice."

Perhaps it is more accurate to say that peoples survive through prudence, power, and justice, and that in order to achieve these goals a critical analysis of the history of one's own people is as important as any analysis of other people's history. In a history of any duration, this analysis will at times be weak or even non-existent, for aspects of prudence, power, and justice vary in intensity of themselves and in relation to one another. A balancing of these elements and a reassertion of analysis will periodically come into view, only to be diminished and, still later, surface again. One can see this dynamic in relation to Deir Yassin: a suffering people committing atrocity; a suffering people trying to end atrocity; those who speak forcefully and those who are silent; one who sees commemoration as movement toward a future of reconciliation and cooperation; another whose immense suffering raises questions to the oppressor which also, though not consciously recognized by him, raises questions to his own people.

Surely we can say that after the Holocaust and the birth of Israel, the liturgy of destruction so hauntingly rendered by Elie Wiesel and others now includes the suffering of the Palestinian people. To be silent, to deflect, or minimize Jewish responsibility for that suffering is no longer possible. Nor can the consequences of such suffering be buried in peace agreements, troop withdrawals, or gala affairs. In the arena of history one can speculate whether Buber's plea to take Deir Yassin seriously would have chastened a new-born state so that Wiesel's celebration of the Israeli victory in 1967 would not have given birth to three decades of military occupation with, among many other violations of human and national rights, the bombing of Beirut in the early 1980s, the Hebron massacre in 1993, or even the 1996 pre-election bombing of southern Lebanon. Could the memory of Deir Yassin, attended to forthrightly, have significantly altered a future of victory and blood? Today that memory of atrocity includes a deep rendering of Jewish history as a path already taken rather than a hypothetical future. In the past Deir Yassin — at least in Buber's understanding — could act as a moment of choice, a choosing of direction. Over time it is clear that Begin's, rather than Buber's, sensibility carried the day. In contemporary Jewish life the memory of Deir Yassin is distant and foreclosed, almost buried under Wiesel's articulation of Jewish innocence. Yet it remains a subversive memory waiting to explode in

Jewish consciousness, a permanent reminder that in the Jewish assumption of power another people has suffered. Jews have and therefore are always capable of committing acts that we lament and rage against when directed against us.

At the same time, Jews are reminded that more than a peace of the powerful and surrender of the vanquished is necessary to come to grips with this history; that acts of reconciliation and justice are possible and necessary even at this late moment. Fifty years after the liberation of the death camps — in fact highlighted at this time — in memorials, museums, restitution, apologies, and confessions are still being made for and to the Jewish people. Could it be that on the fiftieth anniversary of Deir Yassin, similar memorials, museums, restitution, apologies, and confessions will likewise be made at Deir Yassin and in Jerusalem by Jews, including leaders of the Israeli state, to a Palestinian people en route to their belated and necessary empowerment? Memorialization without justice is, of course, an empty symbol that may compound the injury. Justice gives a hearing and meaning to the victims and the possibility of a future that remembers the pain of the past as a difficult road to a place from which a shared life may emerge from what is already a shared tragedy.

Remembrance and the Future

As I reviewed this history and decided to accept the invitation to participate in the memorialization project, I felt a certain ambivalence. Did the emphasis on one atrocity necessitate a recitation of other atrocities, including those committed by Palestinian Arabs in their fight against the Jewish state and later within the context of their forced exile from the land? Could it be that the emergency years of the Holocaust overrode considerations of morality and ethics? The establishment of the Jewish state, made possible in part by Deir Yassin, could thus only come into being with the silence of Ben-Gurion and the narration of Elie Wiesel, a symbiosis that finds Jewish history to be of overriding importance and Palestinian history to be peripheral and secondary. Did I as an empowered Jew in America benefit from Begin's audacity and terror — indeed benefit from the existence and power of the state of Israel? Did I refuse to bloody my own hands and thought by acceding to that extreme violation of human and national rights? Was I a weak diaspora Jew who lacked the will to physically and intellectually fight for my own people? Did remembering Deir Yassin consign all of Israeli history to error and atrocity? And why not condemn the history of all peoples, for does not all empowerment come at some stage through subjugation and atrocity?

Perhaps in the end such a memorial is important less as a resolution of all such questions, or even to minimize ambivalence. Rather, the voices of the dead, forgotten by Jews and now listened to again, remind us of the cost of Jewish empowerment and compel us toward confession and justice. And, as importantly, they serve to rescue the voices of the defeated from history, to at least record their testimony for the future. In Buber's letter to Gandhi, he wrote: "Testimony without acknowledgment, ineffective, unobserved martyrdom, a martyrdom cast to the winds — that is the fate of innumerable Jews in Germany. God alone accepts their testimony. God 'seals' it, as is said in our prayers. Such martyrdom is a deed — but who would venture to demand it?" By remembering Deir Yassin, we as Jews finally acknowledge, make more effective, and observe a martyrdom no longer cast to the wind. Buber continues: "Dispersion is bearable; it can even be purposeful if somewhere there is ingathering, a growing home center, a piece of earth wherein one is in the midst of an ingathering and not in dispersion and from whence the spirit of ingathering may work its way out to all the places of the dispersion. When there is this life, there is also a striving, common life, the life of a community which dares to live today, because it hopes to live tomorrow. But when this growing center, this increasing process of ingathering is lacking, dispersion becomes dismemberment." It is not now incumbent on Jews to apply these words to an ingathering of Palestinians — in terms of refugees, political empowerment, and the sharing of Jerusalem.

There is little doubt of the difficulty that Palestinians have in recognizing the authority of a state that created a martyrdom cast to the winds. It may even be more difficult to pursue peace with political figures who were themselves involved in that process. That those who participate in atrocity later are received as prime ministers and statesmen, even on occasion receiving the Nobel Peace Prize, is startling and instructive. Yet it is these very same people who may ultimately understand their acts and seek in their own lifetime to reconcile them with acts of justice. And though rare, sometimes it happens that a people, recognizing its own imperative for survival, also recognizes its own injustice and seeks to remedy it before it is too late. The assassination of Yitzhak Rabin and the electoral defeat of Shimon Peres give us pause as to whether the lesson has been learned, and whether the architects of the state of Israel, so complicit in the violence against Palestinians, were better able to seek the end of the cycle of violence because they were so integral to it. Their successors, so determined to plead the case of Israel in light of suffering and innocence, may do well to heed the words of Martin Buber, and, even more, his suggestion to honor the dead of Deir Yassin as the first step of his own policy to heal the Jewish and Palestinian people of their traumas. In doing so they could continue the process of replacing injury with hope, displacement with home, thus ushering in the coming millennium with the possibility of peace and justice. Ben-Gurion was silent, and even now the haunting cries of the victims of Deir Yassin echo through history. Here is the possibility of speaking where there once was silence and therefore ending the cycle of destruction which has claimed so many on both sides of the conflict, if only the memory of the Jewish dead includes those who Jews have murdered as well.

On the fiftieth anniversary of Deir Yassin, it is clear that Prime Minister Benjamin Netanyahu has no desire to pursue the shared legacy of death — to honor Jews *and* Palestinians who have fallen victim to a struggle which seems to be without end — and therefore to acknowledge the possibility of shared life. Rather, Netanyahu seeks to expand the physical and rhetorical borders of Israel and Jewish life until those very borders are without markers or memory. But what kind of Jewish life will be lived within these borders? Palestinians will have few places to bury and carry the memory of the dead; Jews will live in a state that in its triumph cleanses the memory of the dead and therefore of culpability as well. The only remembered dead in Israel will be the victims of the Holocaust who will be used, via proxy and irony, to create a future for Jews in the land cleansed of memory of those who originally inhabited it. The dead of Europe will be used to clean the slate of the end of Palestine, *as if a future can be created and sustained for Israel without the memory of the destruction of Palestine.* It is as if Israel can exist without Palestine even as the memory of Palestine is embodied by millions of Palestinians within and around the triumphant state. Could the refusal to remember the destruction of Palestine, illustrated historically in the massacre of Deir Yassin and embodied by millions of stateless Palestinians today, mandate in the future a further cleansing of memory through expansion and even transfer of parts of the Palestinian population? Refusing a historical memorial is simply one step toward refusing to countenance the contemporary markers of the historical and ongoing event of denial and displacement. Could the refusal to commemorate Deir Yassin signal a refusal to end the cycle of ongoing expansion and displacement?

But here we arrive at the question that Buber refused to ask or at least could not answer adequately. Is there a place and time where the state of Israel goes too far, where memory and contemporary life is so abusive that the entire enterprise has to be abandoned? Is there a time and place where a Jew must simply cut ties with the state and the ideology behind it — including the mobilization of the leadership of the world-wide Jewish community, and simply declare oneself an enemy of this project which has so enamored and consumed post-Holocaust Jewish life? Does one remain within the Jewish world and fight from within or declare oneself outside of it and struggle there? As frightening a question is whether energy on such a question even matters at this point of the struggle. For can anything be done now from the Jewish side to halt the expansion, slow the inevitable march, or even reverse the process which insures victory for the Israelis and defeat for the Palestinians? Has Palestine fallen, never to be resurrected in any meaningful sense of the term?

With the negotiated surrender of Palestinians represented by the Oslo accords, the issue of the end of Palestine is hardly theoretical. The interpretative implementation of these accords by Netanyahu further heighten the possibility of this end, even as the negotiations — through political and street confrontations — continue. Negotiating a surrender is through force of historical necessity placing oneself in the hands of the victor; that is, a negotiated surrender is a recognition of a historical defeat and an appeal to the values, ethics, even the mercy of the victor. Surrendering is itself an appeal to the humanity of the victor to recognize in that victory the humanity of the defeated. It is to say that with the end of the battle, a shared future must now be envisioned. Surrender is less an acceptance of a subservient status, than it is the summoning of the dignity to recognize the historical situation and an essential equality with the victor. If the victor will decide the shape of the settlement, the defeated have a place at the table where their humanity must be recognized and dealt with. This was certainly Buber's understanding when he argued for a negotiated return of Arab refugees and when he lectured Ben-Gurion on the recent history of Jewish refugees. For Buber, the defeat of the Arabs did not diminish their humanity, it highlighted it and also proposed a sensibility of reminding Jews what it was like to be on the other side of victory. Surrender, therefore, could be a moment of recognition of a common humanity and a shared history. In this sense, the defeated assume a privileged place in reminding the victor of their own vulnerability and culpability. The decisive moment of history is neither victory or defeat but rather the moment of reflection where both parties meet again in the vulnerability of their mutual humanity and shared history.

What happens when the political and ethical tradition crosses over into militancy and bravado, where the very humanity of the defeated cannot be acknowledged? What happens when the very vulnerability of the defeated ceases to inform the victor of their own vulnerability? When the memory of culpability becomes a place and a mission to be erased? When the language of morality and ethics is so compromised by history that any appeal to such language is derided as weakness or even as traitorous? Of course, there comes a time when such an appeal becomes part of the process of displacement or, as importantly, is unrecognizable in the language and hearing of the imperial state. In this sense, progressive Jews continue in Buber's tradition of dissent and face a situation that Buber could not anticipate. Buber opposed the creation of the state and dissented within it in a language that Ben-Gurion understood quite well even if he ignored it. The success of the state and the rhetoric that accompanies it makes it difficult for the state and its leaders to understand the language of the progressives except in terms of strategic imperatives. The problem today and into the future is less the problem of ignoring the pleas founded on ethics and morality than the existence of a shared universe of discourse which makes that speech understandable. In fact, the progressives have not only narrowed their appeals to ethics and morality, their vision of shared future has narrowed since the time of Buber. Buber spoke of a binational reality in a confederated entity. Today Jewish progressives speak of a separate Palestinian state whose borders are so truncated as to call into question the physical possibility of such a state being a state in anything but name.

What Buber and Jewish progressives have failed to take is precisely the step that needs to be considered in utmost sincerity today, appreciating the difficulty and danger as well as the possibility inherent in such movement. I think here of the need for Jews to come into solidarity with the Palestinian people in the very heart of Palestinian life. That is, the distance maintained by Buber and today by Jewish Israelis like Amos Oz and Jews in America like Michael Lerner must be seen from the perspective of history and contemporary reality as part of the process of displacement of the Palestinian people, or at the very least as a loyal opposition which has lived within and benefitted from that process. Though the hour is late, a further commitment is necessary today: to recognize that a separation of Jew and Palestinian condemns Palestinians to a ghettoized and apartheid-like existence, and that only the inclusion of the Palestinian people in the larger framework of Jewish history, and a renewed commitment to a re-formed and transformed Palestine with Jews and Palestinians as equal partners and citizens, is commensurate to the task ahead. Fidelity to the dispossessed and the dead demands such a reconciliation of past wrongs and the vision of a future worth bequeathing to our children. The closing of the distance between the two peoples is simply the historic and contemporary recognition of a shared life in a shared land and the commitment to transform the sharing from injustice and bloodshed to justice and peace. Of course, this demands a reversal of the process of displacement as that inclusion comes into being. The memorial of Deir Yassin would then be a testament to loss and hope, a memory that witnesses to a renewed life in the very places where the massacres, and by extension the Palestinian exile, began.

Buber faced the question of partition, of the division of Jew and Palestinian. Today we face that same question under Oslo. One wonders if we will fail as Buber did and remain witnesses within a cycle of violence which to this day continues. Could the outcome of this struggle have been different if Buber had crossed over into solidarity with the Palestinian people? Or regardless of what Buber thought and did was the fate of the Palestinians sealed when Ben-Gurion silenced the cries of the victims of Deir Yassin in the ongoing expansion of the state of Israel? Building a state requires energy, action, and a forgetting of the defeated even as one's own victimization is held up as the *raison d'être* of the entire enterprise. Nonetheless, the voices of those who suffered remain to haunt the victorious and to remind them that the cost of victory is high, a cost that may one day call the state into question and herald a new vision of inclusion and justice.

3

The End of Innocence

by Salma Khadra Jayyusi

The 1940s in Jerusalem. The world was at war, but for us school girls, Jerusalem was a peaceful place. Calm, aristocratic, clean and sun-drenched. We were growing up in the most blessed city in the world, a city rooted in history, and we, its children, rooted in its own staunch philosophy of a multi-cultural, multi-religious co-existence.

And the world was my oyster.

I felt my chest fill with joy as my classmates and I crossed the wide street corner leading from the King David Hotel to the Lower Baccaa. At the junction of several streets, at the sidewalk, a black woman always stood, as if she were a fixture of the place; she sold peanuts, freshly roasted in her small, makeshift tin roaster which puffed smoke from a tiny chimney on its side. Always serious and formal, she never made a sign of recognition when we came onto her corner, although we were regular customers. She sold us her peanuts in newspaper cones which she made herself, took our individual piasters and sank back into silence. No one ever knew who she was or when she had come to Jerusalem.

One of us got wind of a mischievous rumor which we whispered to each other, trying to suppress our giggles, that she had another employment at night. Born with a keen sense of aesthetics, I refused to believe that anyone would ever approach such an emaciated, grim, unfortunate woman. "Naive," my classmates told me, "naive, you know nothing of the world!"

My classmates and I used to love walking home from school, chattering and laughing all the way. We had great fun, especially when Margaret Baramki, who was an expert at mimicking the sisters at Schmidt's Girls College, would suddenly start imitating her favorite victim, Sister Irmentraut, the nun who looked after the dormitories, stressing the *z's* for all the *th's* of the English language which Sister Irmentruat mangled, and we'd double up laughing even in the middle of the street. The norm was that young Arab girls should keep complete serenity and modesty, and we were not expected to be so visibly merry in the midst of a major street in the heart of Arab West Jerusalem. Not that it would have been less reprehensible to double up with laughter in Jaffa Street, where the Jewish immigrants to our country had set up their shops; it would have been even more reprehensible for young Arab girls from good families to laugh and make merry in the middle of a Jewish street. It would have been regarded as a capitulation to what seemed to us at the time a very permissive Jewish culture, radically opposed to our cultural standards full of proprieties and strict decorum. We were growing up and our breasts had just started to show voluptuous contours under our uniforms. This dictated the strictest adherence to the rules of good deportment. But who listened? We just laughed and made merry, ate peanuts and forgot about lessons and homework and the even more austere German sisters who tried to teach us humility and the philosophy of hard work.

A few years later, when I had graduated from the American University of Beirut, come back home to Jerusalem and begun teaching Arabic literature at Jerusalem's finest girls' institution, the Teachers' Training College for Girls, which accepted only students who were top of their classes, I would occasionally pass the same corner walking back home, and find the same black woman, grown a little older and a little more shriveled, still selling her freshly roasted peanuts. It seemed natural to see her, to walk those streets which I used to walk with my classmates in slightly younger days, sometimes boisterously merry.

Even then, at that later time, I still did not realize what was really in store for me, or for Margaret Baramki who ended up in Brazil, or for the other equally merry young classmates, plucking joy out of every possible occasion in our spirited adolescence at Schmidts' Girls College in Jerusalem.

Soon after my return home to teach, I became engaged to the man of my choice. Everything seemed right with the world and the world was still my oyster. I had already, as a much younger girl living in Acca (Acre), done what I felt was real service for my country. I instigated and often headed numerous demonstrations even as a girl of ten, and, several times a week, resolutely marched the students, boys and girls, through the streets of Acca chanting anthems and giving hell to the police, until adult Acca was extremely tired of our impulsive patriotic zeal. At Schmidts' Girls College in Jerusalem, however, I concentrated on two main things: first, my lessons, to reward my father for his sacrifice in borrowing money to educate us, as he was, during the first three years of the five year Schmidt period, in a prison camp with no income at all; my second interest was the joy I could get from puns, jokes, riddles, and, occasionally, from serious conversation. Patriotism was kept under the surface, until I shouldered the responsibility of teaching young women at the Teachers' Training College for Girls. It was then that all my upbringing in a home organized around the political agenda of my father, and alive with patriotic feelings of great intensity, came back to me: my father's unrelenting struggle for the Palestinain cause, against the British colonizers, against the Zionist intruders, against the Arab double-dealers; my Lebanese mother's courage, patience, and resistance at my father's side; the whole atmosphere of stress and strife that was the dynamo of our life. I had hardly lived with my father whom I idealized, except during the intervals between prison terms and exile.

At the Teachers' Training College for Girls, I was assigned four classes to teach. The moment I entered the second year class, I saw her. Expressive blue/green eyes, curly hair, a slightly square face that could be lovely when she was not sulking. Slightly overweight. She looked at me shyly and, I felt, a little defiantly. "Something is wrong," I said to myself. Her name, she said, was Hayat Balabseh. "Alright, let's see what you know about Ahmad Shawqi," at that time recognized as the Arab world's foremost poet. She knew very little. Then suddenly, she left the class, looking overwhelmed. Her classmates were sympathetic and in their own cryptic, hesitant way, related a heart-wrenching story. Hayat's father was dead and her mother was paralyzed. She had to look after her and after a younger blind sister. A rich uncle gave them a monthly pittance to help them survive. In short, Hayat was unhappy, tended to sulk, and felt that God had discriminated against her and her sister.

I immediately took her under my wing, and worked on her patiently until I gained her confidence. She was not the child she appeared to be at the beginning. She had a maturity which astonished me. Many were the days when she stayed after school to speak with me of great ideals such as patriotism, duty, charity, and compassion before she hurried to her heavy duties at home.

Then the episode with Miss Marsh and Miss Hecker brought us closer together. I was not much older than my oldest students. I was on duty that day, and one of the classes was inordinately late for lunch. I went to investigate. It was Miss Marsh, the domestic science teacher, who had kept them late without notifying the dining room. When she saw me, she became all fury and behaved rudely. I reminded her that she should have sent word to me, and that it was only proper to be polite. She was terribly angry, and I was angry myself, particularly as she spoke in an uncouth, imperious tone. I left, greatly agitated.

The class refused to continue the lesson, and burst out after me. Miss Marsh went straight to Miss Hecker, the principal. This made the students even more excited, and I could not control them. It became, very quickly, a political confrontation between the British and the Arabs. I heard Hayat say, "They will not speak rudely to us in our own country." Soon enough, Miss Hecker sent after me.

This was the most detestable clash I ever had. I found Miss Hecker furious. "Why have you been rude to Miss Marsh?" she asked imperiously. "On the contrary," I said, "it was Miss Marsh who was rude to me." Then she began speaking about young Arab girls who were anti-British when they should listen to what the British said. "Do you teach your students to dislike the colonizer?" she shouted.

"So you admit that you are colonizers!"

She avoided my question, but shouted, "Tell, me, will you or will you not obey the colonizer? I insist on an answer."

She was mad, but I was madder. "Careful what you say. I will NEVER obey, respect, or recognize the colonizer! Never! I prefer to die first!" I retorted. The students, who were listening under Miss Hecker's window, let out a huge cry.

I stormed out, tears of anger and indignation streaming down my cheeks. The girls met me at the door. "I am off. I will never come back to this infernal place." I took my papers and left, with a horde of day students walking with me, and Hayat carrying my papers and walking at my side. We left an incensed crowd of boarders behind us. Not knowing how to show their anger, they set one of the classes on fire.

I stayed home for a whole week. Hayat visited me every day, trying to soothe my feelings and to persuade me to go back to teach. The dilemma was solved when the highest Arab official in the Education Department, Ahmad Samih al-Khalidi, called me to his office and really calmed me down. My father had been to him, firmly protesting Miss Hecker's aggressive questions. It was clear to me that Ustadh Khalidi had spoken, sternly to say the least, to Miss Hecker. When I went back to teach, she behaved in the normal way, and so did I.

But something had changed permanently at the college. Something precious and venerated had been violated, and the open wound could not be sealed again. From then on, I took every opportunity to tell the girls about the blight which the British had brought on our land.

Miss Marsh suffered a great deal at the hands of the students and the daily workers. But there was nothing that anyone could do to reverse the process. Hayat became a dynamo of patriotism and her classmates often commented on the great change that had taken place in her.

That summer Hayat came to consult me as to whether she should accept a job as a teacher at Deir Yassin. "We need the money, Sitt Salma," she said, addressing me with the Arabic term of respect, tears welling in her expressive eyes. "Mother needs medicines. We can't carry on any longer." It grieved me to see an intelligent young girl throw away her wonderful opportunity to study and guarantee a secure job afterward, in order to earn enough to support a sick mother. I could not give her any advice. For me, learning was a sacred undertaking. I took her to my own mother who already knew and liked her. Mother told her, "Hayat, in every one of us there is a little voice that speaks. Listen to that voice and follow what it tells you."

"It tells me to leave school and teach, Auntie, I have already heard it, but I know Sitt Salma would want me to continue studying."

"Don't listen to Salma." Mother said, "Only listen to that voice."

After she had left, Mother said with a great deal of compassion, "That's a truly courageous girl. You don't find someone like that every day."

I got married that year and left teaching. Hayat came to my wedding that December, and continued her visits to our flat in the Upper Baccaa. She insisted that we visit her at Deir Yassin. This gave my husband and I the opportunity to see the village and to meet many of its people.

The villagers, who seemed to adore Hayat, gave us a sumptuous feast. Many dishes, prepared by the mothers, were carried to her house by her little students, who wanted to honor their teacher's guests. Arab hospitality, unequaled in abundance or grace anywhere in the world, surrounded us. One felt rooted in one's finest traditions, anchored in the belief that, no matter what happened to the world, those ennobling qualities, handed down through the generations, would continue to shield us.

It was a lovely day. The village had handsome stone houses and looked a peaceful, thriving place. The little girls sang patriotic songs, and presented me with a linen center-piece embroidered by the members of Hayat's highest class, each student having embroidered a little, so that it was a collective present made deliberately to honor my visit. In later years, whenever I thought of using this center-piece, I would be overwhelmed by profound sorrow as I remembered their eager faces and their little hands carrying dishes of food and bowls of fruits to us. I still have that center-piece and will leave it as an heirloom to one of my three granddaughters. For years after the massacre, images of those little girls would haunt me.

The last time I saw Hayat was when I was packing to leave Jerusalem for Jordan, where my husband was placed. She looked confident and optimistic. "I shall write to you, if I may," she said. "You must," I said. "I shall send you our address as soon as we are settled."

I never did. That half-year was an unsettled period for me. But I knew, or so I thought, that I would soon be going to Jerusalem, where my parents and family still lived. I never did. The upheaval that dispersed our nation and lacerated our country was almost upon us, and the herald of death lay in wait for Hayat.

When my cousin, the Palestinian historian, Bayan Nuweihed al-Hout heard I was writing about Hayat, she sent me the following note:

> I remember Hayat Balabseh quite well, whom I have known through you. I met her twice, once during that trip with your students, I no longer remember where. Her blind sister was with her,

and that day you insisted that my mother let me go with you.
Mother finally agreed, and I was thrilled by the national songs
sung throughout the bus journey. The second time you brought
her to our home in Jerusalem. She was preparing something for
broadcasting (a talk to be read on the radio). You had been behind
this because she was one of your best students, and, of course, she
was in need. She had to support her mother and blind sister. You
left her in our house and went, and she used my father's library.
She was always smiling, and had a wide ribbon on her hair. When
I saw her sitting at Father's desk writing, I said to myself, 'When
I grow up, I would like to be just like her.'

About her going to Deir Yassin to teach, it was said later on
that it was not easy for a girl to accept a teaching job there, because the village was located near the Jews, but she accepted it
because she had great courage, and needed the money. About her
death, it became very well known that she came out of her house
in her nightgown and started to help people. She was shot and
killed while doing this. I remember a drawing of her: a girl in a
white night gown trying to help an old man....

The first part of this note is Bayan's memory when a little girl of ten.

Survivors of the massacre insist that Hayat could have escaped. In
fact, it was repeated by many that she had already escaped from the
immediate danger area, but had returned to help a wounded man. I
can well believe this.

Her death was my first great sorrow. But it was a sorrow mixed with
anger and a shocking realization that an evil scheme was being enacted against us Palestinians, who despite 30 years of struggle against
Zionist intrigues, were still not experienced enough in the political
sphere. The following months and years were to confirm what had
haunted me at the time as I pored over the events, and listened to what
I felt were banal comments and interpretations by supposedly knowl-
edgeable people, and to marshal songs on the radio that were sicken-
ing to my ears, with Hayat's smiling face constantly before my eyes.
Her face, and those little hands carrying the gift of food to us, the little
hands of the village girls who came walking carefully along the dirt
road that led to Hayat's house, gracefully balancing the dishes lest they
spill.

Oh, those desolate April days after Deir Yassin! Those inconsolable
days! My birthday came and went, and no one noticed. For days I sat in
the same corner, my husband beside me, in silent mourning and con-
templation. Then suddenly it dawned on me:

"How clever!" I said aloud. My husband, sitting next to me looked
horrified.

"Clever?" he asked "What's clever about butchery?"

"The Palestinians will leave. And that's what the Zionists want," I said.

He gave me his full attention. "Yes," he finally said, "but you are speaking of the present. What about time? What will be the repercussions over time? It is not clever at all."

My father-in-law, angry and antagonistic toward these two young graduates thinking they understood the world, bellowed at us: "Quiet you two! No one will leave. We will stand right up to them and give them hell!" My husband winked at me not to go on. I tend to argue everything to its last breath if I feel I am right.

During the following weeks, as floods of Palestinian refugees crossed the borders by land and sea fleeing for safety from possible further massacres, I made it a point not to look into my father-in-law's eyes. I had won a triumph of ideas, at the expense of so much disaster. "We'll soon be back," he asserted. " On the fifteenth of May our glorious Arab armies will enter, and who can stand against them?" He consoled himself and us.

No one slept the night of May 15. There was an atmosphere of feverish expectation that the entry of the armies was going to seal the fate of the Zionist intruders. The whole political web, its very devious intrigues and the clever way it discovered the traitors within and orchestrated their voices and attitudes, was not yet clear to us. With deep sorrow in my heart at the fate of my young friend, and despite the profound doubts the Deir Yassin Massacre created in my mind, I could not but feel some surging hope. Up to the morning of May 16, no one had yet discovered the extent of the enemy's power, and our own impaired assessment of a clever global strategy secretly sealing our fate.

Deir Yassin was the beginning, but also the beginning of the end. The flight of Palestinians from their homes was not due to rosy promises they received from the "invading" Arab armies, but to the realization that they were facing a merciless and blindly vindictive enemy who would stop at nothing to get what they wanted. Rumors had quickly circulated about rape and cold-blooded butchery. Many men sent their women and old folks away and joined the fight, but they had few weapons and almost no ammunition. Day after day the news came in newspapers, and on every Arab radio, of another town or village falling to the Zionists, another confrontation aborted, another Arab army paralyzed in place.

No stranger to this experience can realize the damage which those months did to the Arab soul. No stranger to this experience, living in his or her own sheltered world, can fathom the depth of despair, the grief, the rage of a people wrenched, suddenly, from their long-cherished homes and sent out loose and destitute to the world, so that another people could make a new home in their place. No stranger to this experience can realize what it was to be an Arab at that time, reared in a culture in which shame would leave an indelible mark on a person's conscience, a culture which celebrated virility and honored chivalry and valor, facing now the dishonor of a sudden, unforeseen defeat which cut them off from roots, kin, and country.

I can still hear the crumbling of the barricades of hope and trust, barricade after barricade.

The State of Israel was founded on the soil of Palestine after the most hideous crime in modern times had been enacted against the Jews on European soil. The West, in the face of such insistence on the Holocaust abomination, and being itself the perpetrator, was unable to live with itself, and lost its balance. It became ready to offer a major sacrifice, and the Palestinians were the sacrificial lamb. A warped solution to a moral dilemma of which the Arabs were completely innocent. Neither the ordinary Arab, nor the intellectual will ever be likely to see what many people in the West, compensating for their own guilt, like to see: an absolution for the colossal upheaval Zionism has visited on an innocent people.

Distinct from the many historical antagonists of the Jews all over the world, the Arabs and the other Muslims were the ones who have given them respect and often safe haven throughout the past two millennia, until they built their state on Palestinian expropriated land. Intelligent people everywhere should ask the question: why is contemporary Zionism making its assault against a whole people, and here I mean not just Palestinians but the whole Arab nation beyond, for, regardless of present divisions, the Palestine problem is the Arab world's most harrowing, most enduring dilemma. It is linked in its essence with the memory of a whole national debacle, arousing feelings of shame, notions of failure and inertia, the image of a people at the lowest ebb of their long history. It permeates the whole body of the nation and threatens its integrity. Intelligent people everywhere should ask: how can Israel persist in antagonizing and enraging so many, deceiving and circumventing so many, stirring new hatreds in the hearts and minds of so many, and with persistent aggression, kindling the memory of Zionism's major bloodsheds: Deir Yassin, Qibya, Kufr Qasim, the worshipers at the Hebron Mosque. How can it engage with such a negative, such a senseless, approach those many who will, in 2150, be counted in the hundreds of millions?

I concede: the Arabs now are weak. They have little democracy, no sense of political unity, and some of them, as in all third world nations rising from poverty, colonialism, and bad governments, are often swayed from the selfless patriotic path toward the personal, the material, the trivial. But it would be a weak and puerile imagination that envisaged such a situation enduring for too long. Time, the invariable catalyst, will abort the attempts at keeping this vast Arab world, rich in history, creativity, and civilizational achievements, with one of the longest national memories in the world, in a kind of abnormal fixity. This is a very large Arab world. And it is a world on the move. Though now politically disunited, it has a basic cultural, historical, and social unity which has resisted all attempts at fragmentation. I see these bonds of harmony in every poem, in every novel, in every book of thought. What intellectuals, Islamic thinkers, novelists, poets, and dramatists write anywhere in the Arab world is sought after by all lovers of knowledge and literature from Morocco to Mauritania to the Sudan, to the Arab heartland of Egypt, Syria, Lebanon, Palestine, Jordan, and Iraq, to Kuwait, Qatar, Dubai, Oman, and Yemen. Fragmented, but ultimately of one accord. Disaffected, but basically of the same fiber.

There was a time when it was difficult for the world to recognize the Jewish tragedy. But the tragic memory of centuries of suffering has now been insistently brought forward to the world's attention. Why then when the memory of atrocities inflicted upon the Jews is so strong and vivid, do Zionists insist on being themselves the creators of new atrocities? The Jewish tragedy is a most profound wound, a dagger plunged into the side of humanity. Nothing can assuage it but the gifts of the human heart and mind. Bitterness is not its equal.

Bitterness stands to rob it of its dignity, of the totality of its impact, of its meaning for all, Jews and non-Jews alike.

For in the midst of that soul-crushing adversity stretching over almost twenty centuries, the Jews produced some of the most brilliant minds in many spheres of human endeavor: Freud, Marx, Einstein, and the delightful Spinoza, to name but a few. All of these carried a universal message.

And now, in the midst of the Zionist descent on Palestine, not all Israelis, and not all Jews outside Israel, have complied with the Zionist objective and methods. Some of the most clear-minded, open-hearted speakers for Palestinian rights have been Jews, men and women who could not endure to witness the falsification of reality, the atrocities, the arrogant denials, the contrived induction of arguments, the willed injustice, the ruthless rape of land and lives. They let out a cry which is the most magnificent legacy for the generations of Jews to come; it will certainly combat the arrogant penchant for cruelty and coercion that Zionism and Israel have acquired ever since they thought they could simply kill, evict, imprison, and torture Palestinians and with impunity rob them of life, security, home, and land, of the graves of their forefathers, and the memories of their childhood.

The attempts to contain the message of the Holocaust within the ideological parameters of a Zionist discourse not only undercut the horizon of redemption and freedom, but also the awareness of the universal potentiality for barbarism that the Holocaust represents and which can be unleashed on all.

I can seen how in the midst of the persistent adversity of a people always discriminated against, a deep nostalgia for normalcy and sovereignty will be born. Even with their shorter period of destitution, I saw nostalgia being born in the Palestinian subconscious. Deep longing can become a way of living and feeling, an affective sensibility that pervades a culture. For the essence of longing lies not in its fulfillment, but in its duration. However, you cannot fully regain what twenty centuries have dissipated, what the usual activity of history — migrations, wars, and the constant movement of peoples across the globe — has wrought. You cannot rebuild your shattered lives by following the same methods, attitudes and practices which your oppressors have followed throughout the centuries. Fulfilled longing is longing no more. It nullifies itself. It leads only to deadlock This is why an insistence on the fulfillment of a dream, specifically through intensive aggression and usurpation, culminating in the death or destitution of others, destroys the creative force born out of longing. Longing cannot be abated through crime.

Likewise for the Palestinians now. It is impossible for a people who have known the harrowing experience of these past fifty years, to ever regain their past innocence or feel at peace with a world that has viciously conspired against their freedom and integrity. Their legitimate longing for their status before Zionism transformed their lives into chaos, can never be completely fulfilled.

But this situation cannot last. No one people have remained lords. No one people will remain lords. What took eight centuries in ancient times, and three in pre-modern times, will not take more than a century and a half in the modern age. The world revolves at a breathless speed, and nothing will remain the same. The world is advancing toward a global reciprocity, toward a more intimate knowledge of the other, and so many people, with deeply painful memories of the cruelty, avarice, and belligerent militarism of other bigger nations will, one hopes, stand on the side of the afflicted and, courageously combat the hegemony of the strong, and defeat their ambitions to make of the whole world their own plowing field.

The Palestinians hold their heads high, looking straight into the face of the enemy. These are people who can never be destroyed. They, with other Arabs, yearn for a life of equity and justice. Impediments still clutter the way, but the inner energy and the outer thrust into the world which one sees so clearly in their contemporary cultural output are signs of their forward advance into the twenty first century.

It all depends on how soon the Arabs can benefit from recent experience, and learn the tactics of modern political maneuvers; how soon they can take advantage of the profusion of intellectuals, creative writers, and political thinkers with whom they are so richly blessed; how soon they will rid themselves of their internal cancers.

4

A Jewish Eye-Witness

An Interview with Meir Pa'il

This is a transcript of an interview with Colonel Meir Pa'il, a military historian and a retired member of the Israeli Defense Force, who worked for the Haganah at the time of the massacre at Deir Yassin and who actually witnessed that portion of the massacre which occurred on Friday April 9, 1948. The interview was conducted by Daniel McGowan (with the help of Issam Nashashibi and Allison Hodgkins) at the home of Colonel Pa'il on December 11, 1996 in Tel Aviv.

DM The massacre, as I understand it, took place on April 9, 1948. There are some conflicting reports on when the attack actually began. Some people say that it started at 4 o'clock in the morning; other people say it started later.

MP It was supposed to start at about midnight, but the Irgun and the Stern Gang were not ready. So it started just before dawn, between 4 and 5 a.m.

DM How many people took part in the attack from the Irgun and the Stern Gang?

MP Around 130 people, of whom about 90 were from the Irgun and the others from the Stern Gang.

DM We understand that there was a truck that had a loudspeaker, and that it was to come ahead and warn people of the attack.

MP We call it in Hebrew a "tender." It is a small truck, even smaller than a pickup. It was a small truck with a loudspeaker which they intended to use. But this truck on its way from Givat Shaul to Deir Yassin, a distance of about 300 meters, just at the end of the of the night, turned the wrong way and one of its wheels hit some kind of a hole which was beside the road. The truck path was not guarded by anything, no fence, no trench, nothing. So it just made a mistake and went off to the side, and stood there; no one used it. Anyhow, if you shoot at someone they don't hear any loudspeaker. But regardless it was not employed because the tender did not reach the village.

DM So the loudspeaker was never used?

MP No.

DM I have a map of Deir Yassin from 1945. It shows the village of Deir Yassin, and Givat Shaul close by, and several quarries.

MP This is the truck path, it was not a road, from Givat Shaul to Deir Yassin. This is one kilometer, so you can see that Deir Yassin started here in 1940. The village in 1948 started about here.

DM And from where did the Irgun come?

MP The Irgun came from the southeast, from Beit hak Kerem by foot. They went down to the valley and then climbed up. Their mission was to attack Deir Yassin from the south and to put some light machine guns here on the hill on the southeast side of Deir Yassin. The idea was to hold this hill, to shoot at Deir Yassin, and they were supposed to attack from that side.

DM From the southeast?

MP Yes, from the southeast. The Stern Gang came from Givat Shaul, more or less along the right side of the truck lane; the idea was to attack directly from the east. The Stern Gang succeeded in entering the village. It was daylight. The Irgun didn't succeed taking this part of the village. Then they found themselves joining with the Stern Gang on the east side of the village. They managed after two to three hours to take hold of this part of the village. And the Arab citizens of Deir Yassin took positions here and both sides fired at each other. From the Arab side there were no automatic weapons, only rifles. The Irgun and the Stern Gang had some some light machine guns. And they were shooting at each other (the Arabs from their houses and the Irgun and the Stern Gang from along the road leading into Deir Yassin from the east). Anyhow, they didn't succeed in taking the whole village.

I think you should know that at the beginning of what we call the War of Independence, say from June to December of 1947, the *mukhtar* [village head or mayor] of Deir Yassin met the village head of Givat Shaul and they made a verbal agreement that they would not shoot at each other. They promised that they wouldn't shoot at any Jewish neighborhood, so the Givat Shaul *mukhtar* agreed. Of course he didn't make the agreement without getting the permission of the Haganah [the main Jewish defense organization]. Both *mukhtars* shook hands and both sides kept the agreement until April 9. Two or three weeks before the attack, the Jewish quarters here in Beit hak Kerem, Montefiore, and Givat Shaul heard some shooting near Deir Yassin. In the morning, a group of terrorists from the Iraqi volunteers entered the village of Deir Yassin and the residents drove them out. And the son of the Arab *mukhtar* was killed in this clash. So the people of Deir Yassin kept their word; both sides kept their word.

Prior to the attack, the Irgun and the Stern Gang informed the Haganah that they would attack. The Haganah Chief of Jerusalem, David Shaltiel, didn't find himself able to open fire on the Irgun people and the Stern group, so he said to them, "Okay you do it; we are breaking the agreement. But don't make just a raid; take hold of the whole village and hold it. Because after we break the agreement, after you just make a raid and get out, then the people of Deir Yassin will be able to host some other Arab fighters and then Deir Yassin will become a focal point of trouble for the east side of Jerusalem." They didn't keep their word, and of course no one even raised the issue of massacre, killing people. We knew from Haganah Intelligence Service sources that when the Stern Gang and the Irgun discussed the plan, the Stern Gang put on the table the idea of killing the Arabs, and the Irgun majority and the commander-in-chief of Irgun refused totally to allow it. The idea was to take the village; no one even talked about driving the Arabs out. The idea was to conquer it, and to hold it until the British left the land of Israel. And then insofar as residents of Deir Yassin were quiet people, in this specific situation, like Abu Ghosh, for example, the idea was that they would stay there under Jewish conquest. This is how the plan was formulated. And David Shaltiel asked them to hold the village, because the idea was, that after the British left, the Haganah would build an airstrip for light aircraft, which we in fact did after the British left. For almost a year this strip was used by Jerusalem as an airfield.

DM This map shows several quarries along the road from Givat Shaul to Deir Yassin.

MP There were, and in one of them, on the south side just near the village, the Irgun and the Stern Gang later murdered about 25 Palestinian males. They put them up against the wall.

DM Had they first paraded those males around in Jerusalem and then brought them back there?

MP It was here in the quarry. They had first taken them around Jerusalem in a truck.

DM There are many different reports of how many people were killed. Do you have any idea about the exact number of people killed?

MP There are different reports. The first one was made by the Red Cross delegate, Jacques de Reynier. He entered the village, as far I remember, on Saturday. The attack took place on Friday and according to his assessment, there were around 200 killed. Later, on Saturday evening the two leaders of the Irgun and Stern Gang made some kind of press conference, boasting very much, and they declared that the number of Arabs killed was about 250. This was their own claim. Later they said that they had wanted to boast and that basically the number they gave was not correct. There is an account made by the Haganah commander who had to enter the village on Sunday afternoon, after the Irgun and the Stern Gang had left. He was the commander of the youth troops of the Haganah in Jerusalem. He mobilized about two platoons, around 80 people. And they entered the village and according to their information they could not count the exact number of bodies. They said quite a lot of bodies were burned; quite a lot of bodies were thrown into the wells by the Irgun. As far as I remember, they could count in one place about 70 bodies and in other places about 40, so about 110 were counted in all. But he claimed that this was not the total number; there were bodies that he could not count. Now there is another report in Arabic. According to this report, the number is 110 or 115. I don't know exactly how they arrived at this number. I think there were more than these numbers. Of course, the report exaggerated in some things; for example, it claimed that Jews attacked with tanks, which is totally incorrect.

Remember I was there with the Irgun and the Stern Gang. I entered Deir Yassin just for the sake of watching their military performance without them knowing that I was there.

DM You were there with the Haganah?

MP No, I entered with the Stern group. They didn't notice that. I took one of my soldiers. I was responsible for Special Operations in Jerusalem in those days. So when I was informed that they were planning this, I decided to go along just to watch their military performance. Because no one talked about massacre. But we in the Haganah assessed that sooner or later a Jewish state would be established and these bastards, whom we called "dissidents," would either join the army willingly or they would be compelled to do so. And I just wanted to see their military performance, to assess if they would join the army, what we should do with them, and if they refused to join the army, how difficult it would be for us to overcome them. Their military performance was mediocre. But I found myself watching this massacre without a way to find some commander to tell and to whom to protest. The massacre was stopped, not by me, I was just around, but by the people of Givat Shaul in the afternoon. It was Friday. They entered the village with about 500 people and started shouting, "What are you doing, you bastards, you murderers." This was how it was stopped.

DM We have heard several reports that they used swords or cutlasses or knives, depending on the translation. Is this true?

MP No, all the massacre was done by shooting, either with rifles or submachine guns.

DM Did they use satchel bombs to blow open the houses?

MP No, no. No house in Deir Yassin was bombed. If one would have made an aerial photograph, they would have seen before the massacre, after the massacre, it was the same. No house was blown up. The Irgun and the Stern Gang were not able to conquer the west side of the village. Between Givat Shaul and Deir Yassin, there is today an Israeli industrial area. But to the luck of the historians, the west side of the village is now being used as a mental hospital called the Kfar Shaul Hospital. It is a good remembrance point. To the west you have the Har Nof neighborhood. The Irgun and the Stern Gang did not conquer these buildings which are now the mental hospital. These were at last conquered by a Palmach unit, the elite commandos of the Haganah. After two to three hours of shooting at each other some Stern Gang member ran to the other side of Givat Shaul, because they saw that some Palmachniks were walking there; so he ran there to elicit their help. There was a platoon of 30-35 people with their company commander. They were there on the mountain crest to the north in order to make secure a Jewish convoy which was supposed to come from Tel Aviv on the road below them. So the Stern Gang member went to these Palmach troops and shouted that there is trouble, the Jews are fighting at Deir Yassin, they cannot fulfill their job and they are being killed, please help. The Palmach company commander decided to leave on the Har ha-Menukhot about fifteen people. He took seventeen and a truck and went here through Givat Shaul. And then he placed along the road into Deir Yassin a 2" mortar, a 52 mm. It is a small mortar. And he started shooting, he didn't know the whole story, but for him Jews were in trouble and things happen. So he used the mortar. And he took his people and climbed the hill, and he attacked Deir Yassin from the north side. He made the assault and conquered the whole village in about fifteen minutes with no injury to his men. In this way I could see the bad military performance of the Irgun.

Afterwards I went to him and he told me the story. I saw that the mission was fulfilled, that the village was conquered. I told him, "You know, Jaki, it's finished; get out and find a telephone and tell David Shaltiel the story, so that he will know what happened."

When this small group of the Palmach left, the Irgun and the Stern Gang started the massacre. I couldn't even tell if there was a commander of the Irgun or the Lehi who was directing it or preventing it. It was like a bunch of pogromists, but this time it was not just a pogrom to loot; it was a massacre. Then I started to run here and there. I had a fellow with me with a good camera and I told him to take photos. I couldn't find the room to speak. But I found myself watching this story and until this day I can't overcome my remorse. In the afternoon, the people of Givat Shaul entered Deir Yassin and the massacre stopped. I could see that the dissidents took about 25 males in a truck to Jerusalem and back and they put them in the quarry against the wall and shot them. When I was walking from house to house I could see people dead in the corners — an old man, a wife and two children, here and there a male; it was terrible. We took photos. I left the village just before Friday night and I sent my comrade to take the films; we shot I think two rolls. I told him, "Take the films to the intelligence service. Develop the films but only the negatives, so that no picture will be distributed in Jerusalem." I didn't want it. "Bring me in the morning the two films, developed, but only the negatives." Then I sat in my room and I wrote a report about what I had seen. I had come just to see the Irgun and the Stern Gang's performance. They didn't know how to fight, but as murderers they were pretty good. Until now I cannot see my report. It is hidden, they say, in the Jewish Defense Forces archives.

I am still suffering; I don't like it. Because if at the time I was sufficiently far-sighted, I would have kept the seventeen Palmach people with me, and there would have been no massacre. I would not have let the Irgun and the Stern Gang commit it. I found myself caught in some kind of trap, a psychological trap. I kept my mouth shut for a whole generation. When I got out of the army, I decided to speak out.

DM Do you know if any other photos exist of the massacre?

MP No, unless some people from the Irgun may have taken them. I don't even have what I made. I know that the chief leader of the Haganah read my report and he ordered that my negatives be developed, and he saw the pictures and he showed my report to David Ben-Gurion with some of the pictures. They were angry, totally angry at this performance by the Irgun and the Stern Gang. The Haganah issued a protest, which was published, and I found in it some sentences from my report. And the Jewish Agency apologized with an official letter to King

Abdullah, considering him to be the closest Arab leader. There were no relations with the Palestinians anyhow; there was no Palestinian entity. So they sent a letter, an official one, apologizing, claiming that it was against our wishes.

DM Do you have any idea how many people lived in Deir Yassin before the massacre?

MP We know from the British statistics, that it was considered a small village, having about 700 adults. As far as I know, these were the British statistics; I don't remember exactly. It was considered a small village.

DM We understand that Menachem Begin built his home not far from Deir Yassin.

MP He didn't build his home there. Menachem Begin — to be honest with you, I don't like his political and ideological views, even if I respect him very much for being the Israeli prime minister when we established the peace with Egypt — owned a small apartment in Tel Aviv, not far from the concert hall. When he was elected Prime Minister they gave him a house. He lived there. In 1983, after the bad performance in Lebanon, he decided to resign and everyone understood that he was to some extent mentally ill. At that time, the Israeli government rented for him an apartment here in Yefe Nof across from Deir Yassin and within full view of it. And he stayed there three or four years. And then he was moved back to Tel Aviv, not far from where I live today. And they rented for him another apartment in a more humble, but nice, neighborhood than this. He lived in Yefe Nof for about four years after he resigned from the government. But I don't think that he enjoyed walking there.

DM We didn't know if he lived there on purpose. That gives us a whole different explanation.

MP As far as I know, he was not proud, I tell you. The Irgun and the Stern Gang in Jerusalem performed this terroristic raid without getting permission from their respective centers in Tel Aviv. They did it on their own initiative; you can take it for sure. The top leader of the Stern Gang in those days was Natan Friedman-Yellin. He sent them a letter from Tel Aviv saying more or less like this, "You did it. I am not that proud of it, remembering my family and my Jewish people in Poland." It was published later. Menachem Begin, the leader of the Irgun, did not behave like this. Natan Friedman-Yellin later happened to become a fairly radical dove in Israeli circles. Menachem Begin didn't perform like this. He started boasting and claiming two contradictory versions of the massacre. At first he said there was no massacre; it was bitter battle; we had to fight from house to house, from room to room using grenades and bombing houses. While fighting, we had casualties: four killed, fifteen injured. It was a heavy fight and these events happened to be the outcome of the fight. This is the first version. Later he gave a second interpretation, namely that the Deir Yassin massacre was a very positive performance by the Irgun and the Stern Gang to push forward the Zionist interests in our War of Independence, because after this massacre the Palestinian Arabs were so frightened that it was easy for us to conquer whatever village we wanted. Both versions are total lies. Total lies. In fact the fighting was not that heavy. If they had been good soldiers, they could have conquered the whole village in about an hour, which was demonstrated by the Palmach when they ultimately conquered the village. Regarding the second claim, I examined all the Arab villages and neighborhoods around Deir Yassin in a radius of ten kilometers. I tried to analyze every one of them and answer the question, "Did the Arab residents flee when the Jews approached?" This is nonsense. At first there were some villages which we were unable to conquer. We attacked and were repulsed. So both claims of Menachem Begin are total lies. There was no real fight. And the Arabs were not as frightened as people think. So it is just nonsense. Even so, when he left here, gradually Begin crossed the process of humanization. Because I think in those days, he was a fascist. But gradually in Israel he became milder or nicer, basically. Some of his descendants are still fascists. But anyway, he was a little bit better near the end.

You know the village Ein Kerem. Ein Kerem was easy to take. There were some other places, but I just mentioned those where we had to fight. Every one of them knew about Deir Yassin. And they fought very well, so it was difficult for us to conquer them. And note that we did not succeed in breaking through the wall and conquering the Old City.

DM You mentioned that the Palmachniks used some type of mortar. Was that the famous Davidka?

MP No, no. It was a 2" mortar. It is 52 mm. in diameter. So it was a very small mortar. The British call it a 2" mortar and we call it 52 mm. We still use it. It is a very good mortar for infantry to take a village.

AH Was Yitzhak Shamir at Deir Yassin as well?

MP No, Shamir was not in Israel at the time of the massacre. He was expelled by the British. He was in Kenya, Sudan, or maybe in that moment he was in France after fleeing from some internment camp.

He came back to Israel after the British left. So he was not there. You cannot point a finger at him.

AH You said you thought the massacre began spontaneously.

MP Yes, yes.

AH What concrete examples can you give?

MP I heard shooting. And then I followed the sound of the shooting and I saw that it was made by my people. As far as I could see, there were no orders; there was no one from the Irgun or the Lehi directing them. I know it from our intelligence sources, because the Haganah Intelligence Service had some people who were sent to the dissidents to inform on them. We used the code name "Hassidic."

DM Were there women in the Irgun and the Stern group?

MP There were but I did not notice any women there at Deir Yassin.

DM The French Red Cross worker, Jacques de Reynier, who came after the massacre, said that there were some women and that they had long knives with blood on them. Is that true?

MP Let's put it this way, I was not there on Saturday when he visited. But as far as I assess it, maybe on Saturday some women joined the Irgun and the Stern Gang and you can take it for sure, either for medical service or just to cook something. There was no use of knives when the massacre took place. They just used their sten guns and rifles. As far as I know, they did not even use bayonets, because they had no bayonets anyhow. It was sufficiently cruel without it. There were no rapes. I have seen some Arab reports that there were rapes. There were no rapes. At least I did not see any.

DM Some of the children from Deir Yassin that were orphaned as a result of the massacre were taken to the Old City and later that was the beginning of the Dar el Tifl School, behind the American Colony.

MP Yes? I did not know that. Because what I know, basically, when the shooting started, most Arab males fled Ein Kerem. Then some people went back and they started fighting in the central part of the village. All women and children were left in the village, although some children fled too. After the Givat Shaul people started protesting late Friday afternoon and stopped the massacre, the Irgun and the Stern Gang concentrated about 250 people from Deir Yassin and put them in the school building. There was a school here, you can still find it. You can see "Habad" here — near here, just that side of the road. You can still see it; it says Habad Synagogue. It was a small school, composed of two small classrooms, and its size is another indicator that this was a small village. The dissidents concentrated in these two rooms about 250 people, children, women mostly. And they surrounded the building claiming they would bomb this schoolhouse on their heads. And the people of Givat Shaul shouted at them, "Don't do it, you murderers."

AH So what you are saying is that the Irgun and the Stern Gang put close to 250 people in this schoolhouse and...

MP They were just going around the building threatening that they would bomb it.

AH Were they prepared to?

MP I did not see any explosives there. Then they brought four trucks and put these people on them and they drove them through Givat Shaul and through the Morasha neighborhood near Damascus Gate.

IN What is the possibility of getting a look at your report with the photos?

MP Even the head of the Haganah in those days, to whom I sent this report, was not allowed to see it. Afterwards, he directed them to put it in the archives.

IN But this is 48 years later.

MP Tell them.

IN Do you think that if someone asks again today that he will be rejected?

MP Try. You have an association. Send a letter to the minister of defense, or to the prime minister, an official nice letter, saying that you know that there are some reports, which until now have been kept secret. Would they be kind enough to let you see them; they are in Hebrew, of course.

DM What date did you send your report?

MP I wrote it during the night between Friday and Saturday. I gave it to David Shaltiel on Saturday, the 10th of April. And I imagine that it took several days to be sent to Tel Aviv because there were convoys on April 13 that came from Tel Aviv. Some of the convoys went back. Or he could have sent it by air; we had an airstrip not far from Rehaviot. I don't know exactly. But I know he saw it, and his written report was shown to Ben-Gurion.

AH What became of the residents of these other villages that you were describing?

MP There are some Christian families, especially Christian entities in Ein Kerem, Abu Gosh, which is a very interesting site. The Arabs, the Palestinians are still there but were moved two kilometers toward the south.

All the other Arabs of the corridor between Tel Aviv and Jerusalem, which we managed to conquer, fled or were expelled. Additionally, we considered them enemies. They used to shoot at our convoys on the roads.

DM Concerning the final remains of the dead. Were they buried or burned?

MP They were buried and burned and thrown into the wells. This was the most convenient system of how to do it. To throw them into wells, and then to cover the wells with stones and dirt.

DM Have you ever been back to Deir Yassin?

MP Yes, more than once. I even take my students there. The Irgun and Stern Gang don't like me going there. I take them there, because I think we should see it and know it. To your good luck, they decided to establish a mental hospital in the central buildings of Deir Yassin. If it was not for that, maybe by now there would not be any houses left; the entire neighborhood of Har Nof would cover all of it. And this industrial quarter here would have expanded to Har Nof. I consider this mental hospital as a good remembrance point. It is a very interesting hospital and has a very original system of management. The residents run it themselves; they have a committee of the people.

DM And it is surrounded by a fence, so it is self-contained.

MP It's not a fence, like in an internment camp. It's a village. It's open; the gate it totally open; everyone can go in and out. Of course, I am not an expert, but I know that it is considered a very liberal system.

IN You mentioned Jerusalem as one of the examples of the places, such as the Old City, which could not be conquered in 1948. Were you involved in that?

MP No, we succeeded just once to break in, after the British evacuated, through the Zion Gate. We succeeded in occupying a position outside the wall. Then we managed to break in through the Zion Gate to the Jewish neighborhood and then we were repulsed from the gate. There was some kind of mistake around this gate. And when the Arab Legion entered the city, the gate was not held by the Jews and the Arabs took it. So the Jewish neighborhood was re-encircled and cut off. This happened to be our only success through the Zion Gate.

But, when we conquered the Old City in 1967, we came from the Lions Gate. And another group entered through the Dung Gate.

AH You said you were here from before dawn. And the massacre took place over how many hours?

MP It started around twelve. After the whole village was conquered. From about 12 until about 4 or 5 p.m.

AH So in those four hours, why wasn't it possible to bring someone to stop it?

MP I went here and there. I didn't know even one of the dissidents. Anyhow, it's a fact. I just regret letting the Palmachniks get out, for if they would have stayed there, I think we could have avoided or stopped the massacre.

Don't think that the Irgun and the Stern Gang stopped thinking about putting *their* memorial here at Deir Yassin. Because some of them are still proud of it.

If I were the prime minister, I would offer a compromise: to put on the very same site two memorials. There would be an Arab point of view, different Jewish points of view, my point of view, and the previous establishment's point of view, the existing establishment's point of view. It would be interesting. It's a good idea.

5

Assault and Massacre

by Sheila Cassidy

Two disasters broke the back of the Palestinian resistance during the first ten days of April 1948 to the drive for a Jewish state: the death of Abdul Qader Husseini at Kastel, and the massacre of the villagers at Deir Yassin. The loss of Husseini at Kastel deprived the Palestinians of the required leadership just when they needed it the most. The discovery of his body by the Arabs after they had retaken Kastel caused them to lose heart, such was their faith and dependency upon this scion of one of the most prominent families of Palestine.

It was the day of Husseini's funeral in Jerusalem when the grisly discoveries started surfacing from the massacre of Deir Yassin. The village of stone cutters had been attacked by the Irgun and Stern Gang in the dawn hours of April 9, 1948. They were accompanied by a Haganah member, Meir Pa'il, there to assess their military capabilities.

An Irgun force had set out from the Beth Hakerim Quarter to assault Deir Yassin from the southeast. The Stern Gang unit that Pa'il was with attacked from the east. A truck with a loudspeaker, that was to be used to warn the villagers to flee their homes, stuck in a ditch instead, the message never to be heard.

Meanwhile, the invaders were spotted by the sentries in the village as the Jews made their way up through the *wadi* [stream bed]. A shot rang out, and then another. "Ahmed! *Yehud alainou!*" The sleeping village awoke. Those that could, threw on whatever clothes they could find and fled hurriedly to the west. Many were barefoot. Those that stayed, prepared to defend the village.

A machine gun opened up at the edge of the village. The Irgun and Sternists started to advance. Confusion reigned. This should have been easy. The village was at peace with its Jewish neighbors and had reportedly run some Arab fighters out so it would not be used as a base. It was also Friday, the Muslim Sabbath.

The remaining villagers began a spirited defense of their homes. They had only old mausers and Turkish rifles from World War I. Attacking Irgun and Stern Gang members were surprised by the tenacious resistance. No one had experience in house-to-house fighting. As the morning wore on, the Irgun and Stern Gang became more unnerved. The attack stalled.

A Palmach unit was stationed on the crest of a mountain to the north to secure the route of a Jewish convoy due to pass by on the road below them. One of the Sternists saw some of them walking around and went to ask their help. The Palmach unit had a machine gun and a two-inch mortar. Its commander divided up the unit, leaving about half to watch for the convoy and brought the remaining seventeen and a truck through Givat Shaul to the village. His men set up the mortar along the road and began to fire into the village. The commander took his men along the north side of the road. They climbed the hill and attacked. Resistance was silenced by noon.

Jamil Ahmed, who lived near the edge of the village, remembered the day his village died. During the battle he watched in horror as first his cousin, Youssif, and then his brother, Issa, along with several friends, were killed. "They took them as prisoners, raised their hands, and took them to the edge of the village near my house and sprayed them with gunfire. A blind man was also shot like that. A child, seven years old, was also killed that way. Other women were taken prisoner and put into trucks. I was in my house, carrying a gun, defending the village. It was an old rifle from World War I, British." He managed to flee the village at noon, going to the nearby village Ein Kerem.

After taking the village, the Palmach men left. The attack had cost the Irgun and Stern Gang four dead and 35 wounded. Incensed at the losses, the attackers fell on the luckless village.

They began the "cleanup operation," going from house to house, first spraying bullets and then throwing in grenades. It mattered little who was in the houses. Men, women, and children were brought out of other houses, lined up against the wall, and shot. Savagery increased with each villager's death. Haleem Eid saw her sister Sahliya shot in the neck. Sahliya was nine months pregnant. The murderer cut the dead woman's stomach open with a butcher's knife. Another woman, Aiecha Radwas, was shot as she tried to save the baby.

Mohammed Jaber, home because his school had closed early, watched the scene play out from under his bed. He saw "Jews break in, drive everybody outside, put them against the wall and shoot them. One of the women was carrying a three-month-old baby."

Twenty-five men were brought out of the houses, loaded onto a truck, and paraded through the streets of Mahneh Yehude and Zikhron Yosef Quarters in Jerusalem, in Roman triumph. Then they were taken to a stone quarry between Givat Shaul and shot in cold blood. Women and children were forced onto a truck, paraded in Jerusalem, and released at the Mandelbaum Gate.

The next day the Arabs called Jacques de Reynier, the Swiss-born representative of the International Red Cross, and asked him to go to Deir Yassin. He asked the Jewish Agency and the Haganah about Deir Yassin, but neither organization responded. They said the territory was held by the Irgun, refused to help him, or even be responsible for his safety. So de Reynier made his own arrangements and set off.

He arrived in Deir Yassin to find the Irguns still doing "cleanup operations," brandishing all manner of pistols, machine guns, hand grenades, and knives. He looked inside some of the houses. The "cleanup" had been done with machine guns and grenades. "It had been finished off with knives, anyone could see that."

The only people that de Reynier found alive were a six-year-old girl, a grandmother, and a dying man. He arranged for the ambulance to take them to the hospital.

That night, in his diary, he wrote: "The first thing that I saw were people running everywhere, rushing into and out of houses, carrying sten guns, rifles, pistols, and long ornate knives... They seemed half mad. I saw a beautiful young girl carrying a dagger still covered in blood. I heard screams. The German member of the Irgun explained, 'we're still mopping up.' All I could think of was the SS troops I'd seen in Athens."

Two days after the massacre, the Irgun had disappeared, and the Haganah were still trying to deal with the carnage.

At first Deir Yassin was destined to become an airfield. A year later, religious Jews founded Givat Shaul Bet on the lands of Deir Yassin. President Chaim Weizmann sent written greetings, and the chief rabbis took part in the statement festival. In 1980 some buildings were bulldozed as a prelude to a settlement of Orthodox Jews. Streets were named after the Irgun and Sternists who took part in the attack. More recently, most of the cemetery was bulldozed for a new highway. The actual site of the village is now a mental hospital, about 1500 yards from the Jewish Holocaust memorial, Yad Vashem. Most of the stone houses still remain, mute testimony to the fury that enveloped them almost 50 years ago.

In 1967, after the Israelis overran the West Bank, Jamil Ahmed returned to his old house in Deir Yassin. The hospital guards had not wanted to let him in. He found his house being used as an administration center. After he and his son, Ziad, visited his uncle's grave, they drank water from their old cistern. "It was like my whole heart and all my life were all lost in that moment when I went and saw."

6

The Surviving Children of Deir Yassin

by Pat McDonnell Twair

As hostilities intensified between Jews and Palestinians during the spring of 1948, Hind Husseini, who coordinated the establishment of Arab children's' centers in Jerusalem, found it increasingly difficult to move about the war-torn city. The morning of April 9 had resounded with volleys of gunfire marking the solemn funeral of her cousin, Abdul Qader Husseini, the charismatic leader of the Palestinian resistance. He had died the day before in a six-day battle to regain Kastel, an Arab fortress overlooking Jerusalem. Now this most revered of all Palestinian fighters was being buried at the sacred Haram al-Sharif. This was the biggest blow the Palestinians had so far sustained. As the Palestinians stopped shooting their precious bullets into the air and began to mourn the sudden loss of Abdul Qader, ominous rumors began to spread of a massacre. The atrocities mentioned in whispers were more horrible than the bereft Arabs could comprehend and they seemed to be taking place that very morning on the western outskirts of the city near Kastel.

A few hours later, Arab authorities announced Jewish terrorists had attacked the village of Deir Yassin. In hope of inciting neighboring Arab governments to come to their aid, they graphically described the slaughter of Deir Yassin's civilian inhabitants. The Arab governments did not respond, but tragically, the Palestinian peasants did and began to make a mass exodus from their homeland of millennia to the Jordanian border.

Hind huddled close to the radio in her two-room apartment in the Suq al-Haman neighborhood of East Jerusalem. She realized a massacre of this magnitude meant all out war. She did not go to her office the next morning as coordinator for the Arab Women's Union. However, when the level of gunfire sporadically abated, she ventured outside. Turning the corner, the horror of the massacre of Deir Yassin hit her full force as she beheld several bloodied children huddled against a wall.

"Oh my darlings, what happened? Are you hurt? What is this, you have no shoes, why are you in nightclothes?"

The shivering children were too frightened to cry, they stared at her in wide-eyed horror unable to describe the atrocities they had witnessed.

Picking up the two youngest, Hind gently whispered to the dirty, frightened children to follow her. It was bitterly cold even at midday on that April 10 morning. Hind unlocked the door of her apartment and motioned to the frightened waifs to follow her inside. She gently lowered the toddlers onto her bed, rushed to bring blankets from a closet and began to heat water for bathing.

Now that they knew they were safely in the hands of an adult who spoke Arabic but dressed differently than the women of Deir Yassin, the children began to whimper. Mohammed, the oldest, told Hind that he had hid under his parents' bed when the terrorists entered his home. He had heard his mother scream for a long time. From his hiding point, he had seen the bodies of his sisters and brothers fall to the floor. The house had been looted. Several times hands had pulled out old clothes and shoes from under the bed, but he had not been detected. For the rest of the day and into the night, the little boy had heard groans and cries, gun shots, screeching tires, and the strange guttural shouts of the intruders. At daybreak the bodies that lay in his house were pulled out. When he saw his mother's lifeless body being dragged by its heels like a sack of wheat, sobs uncontrollably came out of his throat. A terrorist reached under the bed, touched him, pulled him from his hiding place, and roughly walked him to a truck where several other children were holding on to one another.

One eight-year-old girl was soaked in blood; Mohammed feared she had been wounded. He didn't want her to die in this truck. Barely able to speak, she told him her name was Thoraya and assured him she wasn't wounded. Her aunts had protectively hid her behind them when the terrorists entered their house. The women had been stabbed, their gold earrings and gold bracelets forcibly removed, but Thoraya had remained safe and protected by their bodies that fell over her and which she felt stiffen over the hours. It was only when one of the terrorists returned to make sure all the jewelry had been removed from the corpses that she had been found and taken to the truck.

Hind bathed Mohammed and dried him with a warm towel. Then grasping his arms inside her tightly clenched fists, she looked directly into his eyes and pledged: "You will never, ever be alone again, I swear."

For the ensuing week, Hind worked with Adnan Tamimi to locate the surviving children of Deir Yassin — 55 in all. In light of the brutality of the attack by the Irgun and Stern Gang militias, it was surprising to some that so many had been spared. Trucks had dispatched the children to the Muslim quarter where they had been dumped on street corners.

Long before the massacre of Deir Yassin, which would become the major milestone in her life, Hind had put aside thoughts of marriage as she watched her homeland crumble under the onslaught of European Jews. The Husseini family of Jerusalem was about as close to aristocracy as Islam recognizes. Her father, a judge, had died when she was two years old. Being the only daughter in a family of five boys, she was pampered to the extent of preparing to pursue a higher education, but protected in the sense that it was deemed unwise for her to attend a university in Europe with World War II approaching. After she completed high school at the English College for Girls in Jerusalem in 1937, she began teaching at the Islamic Girl's School. She again broke with tradition when she left the family compound to live in her own apartment after she accepted a post in 1945 with the United Women's Society Organization.

Now this pioneer Palestinian feminist realized it was time to return to the family home with her 55 babies. She had only 135 Palestinian pounds in the bank, but Hind wrote in her journal: "I will live with these children or I will die with them."

Hind's family was sympathetic to her calling. They turned over to her the elegant Dar Husseini (Husseini House), a house her grandfather had built in 1891 and in which she had been born on April 25, 1916. So on her 32nd birthday, just two weeks after the massacre of Deir Yassin, Hind renamed the stately mansion Dar El Tifl (Children's House).

Thereafter, construction seemed always to be going on in the compound. Two four-story buildings were built, schoolrooms were opened in standing structures. Teachers and yet more teachers were hired. Orphans were rarely turned away.

In 1963, Hind determined she should learn the very latest in educational skills and attended the University of Hamburg for three years.

Concerned that Zionists were attempting to undermine the history and culture of the Palestinian people, the dedicated nationalist found another passion: the preservation of Palestinian arts and crafts. She began collecting pottery, old furniture, and vintage hand-embroidered dresses; she participated in many symposia in neighboring Arab states that dealt with Palestinian handicrafts. Eventually Hind established a folkloric center and museum exhibiting baskets, inlaid furniture, brassware, and national costumes of the Palestinian people.

Over the years, Hind remained steadfast in ignoring offers of millions of dollars for her property in the traditionally upscale Arab neighborhood of Sheikh Jarrah. Shortly before her death in 1995, she took the ultimate step to protect it by registering it as a possession of the Waqf (the Islamic religious authority).

Today 250 orphans live at Dar El Tifl and 1,450 day students receive instruction from preschool to graduate level studies. All high school graduates have excellent English skills. The high standards of the curriculum and staff have earned a prestigious academic record for the school. Conscious that not all students are destined for higher studies, Hind established vocational training in such subjects as catering and secretarial work. A new science workshop is being overseen by two Palestinian professors living in California for 20 gifted students between the ages of thirteen and fifteen years. Working on five computers, students carry out experiments in fluid dynamics, genetics, and physics. Primarily working with materials around them — grocery bags and bottles — they have created a model submarine and hot air balloon. Dar El Tifl students will be on the Internet in 1998. Two years ago the Hind Husseini Art and Literature College was established on the compound and offers bachelor's degrees in English, Arabic, and social studies. Dar El Tifl shares supervision with Al Quds University over a master's degree in Palestinian and Islamic civilization. The original family residence now houses a primary health clinic and guest quarters downstairs while administrative offices are upstairs.

Yet, 50 years after the massacre at Deir Yassin, Dar El Tifl is suffering more than ever at the hands of extremist right-wing Israeli Jews bent on taking over all of Jerusalem. Orient House, the unofficial headquarters of the Palestinian National Authority in Jerusalem, has been the special target of the Jewish settlers who brought Benjamin Netanyahu into power as prime minister in June 1996. Orient House is directly across the street from Dar El Tifl, and Israeli militants often break onto the school grounds and threaten students as they approach the school.

Teachers and students alike have received hope from the United States since 1992 when Dalal Muhtadi, a Saudi citizen who lives in California, founded Dar El Tifl-USA. "I had wanted to assist needy Palestinian children for years," Muhtadi explains. "Then in late 1992, my Auntie Hind called from Jerusalem and said she needed my help."

Over the years, the Saudi government had made grants to Dar El Tifl, but these had dried up after the Gulf War. Muhtadi traveled to Jerusalem, talked to Hind Husseini, the directors and teaching staff and familiarized herself with the school curricula and operation of the orphanage.

"I was convinced Dar El Tifl was accomplishing the goals it had set for itself. Now it was my turn to muster support for it in the United States," continued Muhtadi, a great-niece of Hind Husseini.

But, why, we asked, would Israeli extremists want to terrorize Palestinian orphans. Hasn't enough blood been shed over the past half-century?

"They don't hide their motives," Muhtadi replied. "Fundamentalist fanatics in Israel want to wipe out every trace of a Palestinian presence in Jerusalem."

Mean-spirited settlers do their best to make life miserable — even scary — for Dar El Tifl students. Settlers have broken the gate of the school, entered the playground area, and threatened children. In their protests against Orient House, fanatic settlers have installed themselves in front of the school and raised wooden signs painted with a skull and crossbones on the school wall. When day students approach the school, shouting settlers with raised firsts make them walk a gauntlet of insults and loud curses.

Mahira Dajani, who heads Dar El Tifl's board of trustees, writes: "We have tried to teach our children the love of peace and to train them to accept peaceful coexistence as a reality and to forget the evils of war. The presence of settlers outside the school gate changed the children's outlook on life as a whole. The settlers harassed the children in many ways, including: uttering filthy words and making lewd gestures, throwing rotten fruit and empty bottles at the school gate and inside the school grounds, and trespassing on the school grounds repeatedly so that the school has been forced to erect a wire fence over the wall."

The Israeli military also has intensified its presence in front of Orient House since Netanyahu's election. Dar El Tifl's school wall has become a favorite place for Israeli troops to stand, thus imposing a siege mentality on the children in the playground. School officials complain the tear gas the soldiers use has an unpleasant smell. But the bad odor is nothing compared to the stench of urine. Portable latrines have been set up in front of the school for the soldiers' use, but they relieve themselves throughout the area. The Palestinians believe this is a deliberate insult and provides a frightening spectacle to young girls on their way to school.

"You can't imagine how terrible it is," Muhtadi commented. "The urine odor is overwhelming for a three-block radius."

Many day students have transferred to other schools rather than be chased and threatened by nasty settlers. The Israeli policy of making Jerusalem off-bounds to West Bank and Gazan Palestinians has left students from these areas with one of two choices: either to become boarders at Dar El Tifl and seldom be with their families or transfer to schools in Gaza or the West Bank.

The school also has lost those of its teachers who live on the West Bank, because Israel won't grant them identity cards to enter Jerusalem.

What are the circumstances of the children who live at Dar El Tifl? Two such youngsters are Sabreen, 5, and Wafa, 15. Sabreen's father was shot and killed after he finished his prayers at a mosque in Gaza. At the time, Sabreen's mother, who has twice undergone surgery for a heart condition, was pregnant with her third child. She had no choice but to leave Sabreen at Dar El Tifl. Wafa is from Bethlehem, where her mother was shot dead by Israeli bullets while she was shopping. Wafa's father is unemployed. Rather than have his children starve, he brought Wafa and her two brothers and two sisters to Dar El Tifl.

Despite the racist behavior of the settlers, Dar El Tifl continues to heal and educate. Each year since 1950, some 800 Palestinians have graduated from the institution. Funds from Dar El Tifl-USA have established a counseling center where a social worker, a graduate of the Hind Husseini College of Art and Literature, works with traumatized students and refers those with special needs to professional care-givers.

Postscript

Immediately after the death of Hind Husseini in September 1995, Muhtadi announced a memorial would be given in her home in Yorba Linda, California. Word spreads as fast among the Palestinian community of California as it does in the homeland and dozens of people whose lives had been affected positively by Hind came to Muhtadi's home.

"I shall never forget it," Muhtadi recalled, "when an older couple entered the living room. The woman said 'I am one of the children of Deir Yassin.'"

It was Thoraya, who years earlier had married Muhammad, and together they had had four children.

For most of that evening the couple recalled the traumatic events of April 9 and 10 and their rescue by Hind.

They left that night for their home in San Diego. Muhtadi has never since been able to find them. Their phone was disconnected. Messages left at their children's homes were never answered. The tragedy of Deir Yassin has left deep scars that will last for generations. Nonetheless the vision of Hind Husseini has given hope to many who were beyond hope as later Israeli onslaughts left their toll of traumatized, orphaned Arab children.

7

A Memorial Landscape Design for Deir Yassin

by Fuad Bassim Nijim

In 1948, Deir Yassin, a Palestinian village of about 750 people, was one of the first villages to be attacked by Jewish terrorist groups in Palestine. The attack took place early in the morning of Friday April 9, 1948. By noon over 100 people were killed, half of whom were women and children. Twenty-five young men of the survivors were loaded into trucks, paraded through the Zakhron Yosef quarter in Jerusalem, then taken to a stone quarry between Givat Shaul and Deir Yassin and shot to death. The remaining residents were trucked away to the eastern part of Jerusalem. In his book, *Terror Out of Zion*, J. Bowyer Bell quotes Yeshurin Schiff, a Haganah commander, as saying: "It was a lovely spring day. The almond trees were in bloom; the flowers were out, and everywhere there was the stench of the dead, the thick smell of blood, and the terrible odor of the corpses burning in the quarry."

While many in the world community have not heard of the massacre at Deir Yassin, to this day the name and incident resonate loudly and deeply among the Palestinian people who are haunted by its magnitude and feel the loss. The massacre spread a shock wave of fear across Palestine. It caused a mass exodus of Palestinians fleeing into eastern Palestine, Jordan, and Lebanon.

Deir Yassin sits on a hilltop approximately three miles west of the Old City of Jerusalem. When one visits Deir Yassin today, one finds an Orthodox Jewish community that literally lives over the dead. It is ironic to see right outside the window of a house now occupied by a Jewish family a tombstone marking the grave of a Palestinian. In the same way, it is unnerving to look straight south from Deir Yassin. The next hilltop hosts the buildings of Yad Vashem, the Holocaust memorial and museum of the Jewish people. If one visits Yad Vashem, goes through its hallways and experiences its deep and troubling message, one exits facing north and looking right at Deir Yassin. For those who don't know, Deir Yassin becomes a community lost in time and space. But for visitors who know the history of Deir Yassin, the irony becomes breathtaking.

Were the ghosts of Deir Yassin ignored or simply bulldozed over? When Yad Vashem was dedicated, did the ceremonies include a mention of Deir Yassin? Or was there silence? The idea of a Jewish memorial began as early as 1942, but it was not until June 1, 1947 that the first plenary session convened — less than one year before the massacre at Deir Yassin. The Israeli Knesset passed the Law of Remembrance of Shoah and Heroism —Yad Vashem on May 18, 1953, only five years after the massacre at Deir Yassin. While some Jews spent over ten years planning a memorial for victims of the Jewish Holocaust, Palestinians were pushed into homelessness and exile, often at gunpoint. Although Yad Vashem was built, no memorial was ever built for the massacre at Deir Yassin.

This project is a development of a possible landscape design for a Palestinian memorial at Deir Yassin. My essay has the following sequence: First, I start by drawing a picture of Palestinian life before 1948. Second, I relate my family's suffering in Jerusalem during the 1940s. Third, I describe my proposed design connecting its concept to sixth century architecture of the eastern Mediterranean. I also contemplate how and when a Palestinian memorial would be built. Fourth, I explain a visitor's walk through this memorial landscape, including a description of the symbolism attached to this walk. Fifth, I reflect upon the importance of a Deir Yassin memorial, after which I reflect on a possible future for the village of Deir Yassin. I conclude my chapter hoping for a different relationship between both peoples based on God's equal love for all peoples in every land.

Palestinians Before 1948

Before 1948 Palestinians lived in their own homes, villages, and towns, and among family, friends, and neighbors. They had their own farms, schools, and hospitals. There were also larger towns and trade centers like Jaffa, Gaza, and Jerusalem. Palestinians had their own music, poetry, and pride. As an agrarian society, Palestinians depended mainly on farming their land. Unlike claims to the contrary, Palestine was not arid, but abundant with farms that produced crops like olives, almonds, lemons, oranges, tomatoes, and lots of *kusa* (squash). Palestinian families pride themselves on eating from the blessings of their own land. This continuous and tranquil life helped preserve ancient traditions, such as al-Sahjeh dance performed at weddings or the cross-stitch embroidery that is specific to regions within Palestine while unique in its character and style. Foods like the Jerusalem salad or the farmers' salad are also part of this Palestinian culture. These traditions and customs were passed on from parent to child to grandchild. This predominantly Arab heritage and identity generally unified Palestine's diverse communities.

This identity, however, was challenged early in the twentieth century with the accelerated immigration of European Jews into Palestine. This immigration built tension and intense mistrust of the European Jewish immigrants whose goal was to create an exclusively Jewish state. Palestine lived through its infamous troubles of the late 1930s, but tension continued leading to conflict and culminating in the 1948 war.

Palestinians were horrified at the prospect of dividing their country into two states as called for by the United Nations partition plan of November 29,1947. At that time, Christian and Muslim Palestinians comprised about two thirds of the population and owned about 94 percent of the land. Canon Naim Ateek of Jerusalem likens the Palestinian reaction to the partition plan to that of the true mother of the infant that King Solomon suggested be cut in half to settle a dispute between two mothers. The escalating events leading to and including 1948 were like theft in the night that stripped away Palestinian farms, villages, and pride, making them homeless in the universe. Building a memorial is but one small step towards bringing back the humanity of people who lost too much too fast.

Other massacres took place in Palestine during the war of 1948. That time was catastrophic to all Palestinians, including my family. At that time, my father, Bassim, was living with his family in al-Musrara neighborhood of Jerusalem. My grandfather, Khalil, was an attorney working in the court houses of the Palestinian government. The following two incidents that happened to my family depict the impact of the war of 1948 on the Palestinians.

On Wednesday October 31, 1945, my father, then seventeen years old, along with my uncles Ibrahim and Badie, nineteen and nine years old respectively, and my aunt Bushra, twelve years old, were on a train returning to Jerusalem from a visit to their aunt Badia in Ramleh. About ten minutes into the journey, Jewish terrorists disguised as passengers pulled the emergency stop. Other armed terrorists waiting on the ground joined them and started shooting to scare passengers into fleeing the train. Many were able to escape, but those who couldn't were forced at gun point to lie on the ground face down while the terrorists pulled away the locomotive and then set the train on fire. My father and his siblings were part of the unfortunate crowd that witnessed their train being set on fire. Then, in a split second, the terrorists vanished, leaving a large crowd of Palestinian passengers on their own in the countryside. The four siblings had to walk all the way back to Ramleh to Aunt Badia's home.

This incident was but one of a larger attempt by Jewish groups to disrupt the railway system of Palestine. That same day, as Menachem

Begin wrote in his book *The Revolt*, there were about 500 explosions targeting 186 points on the railway lines. Railway traffic was suspended throughout Palestine, including the Lydda-Jerusalem line that my father and my uncles were on. Unlike Begin's claim to the contrary, my Uncle Badie remembers hearing of many injuries, including fatalities, particularly that explosion on the Lydda-Haifa line. My father and uncles were fortunate to have been on a train with no passenger fatalities.

Those attacks were a sign of things to come. Al-Musrara is less than three miles from Deir Yassin, and news of the massacre there sent shivers of fear into the hearts of every Palestinian man, woman, and child. When my grandmother Bassima once heard someone yelling, "the Jews are coming," she fainted out of fear. The 1948 fighting had already erupted and two bombs fell inside the garden of my grandfather's house. Glass was shattered and a good part of the roof shingles were broken, but luckily no one was injured. Uncle Badie recalls, "a time of constant turmoil, and people were in a state of continuous panic." Al-Musrara was defenseless so my grandfather, Khalil, took his family to hide inside the walls of the Old City. They found refuge in one room at Dar el-Adra. Carrying only very few items, my family left all its belongings — furniture, clothing, and food — in their home at al-Musrara. A Jew from Eastern Europe occupied and claimed my family's home, including our furniture and clothing. To this day, we cannot go back to claim our home or our belongings. Most Palestinians lost homes, livelihoods, and communities this way. There were numerous United Nations resolutions calling for Palestinian compensation and repatriation, but these resolutions were ignored.

By June the fighting and atrocities reached huge proportions. All of Palestine was in turmoil. In July the United Nations called for a truce to be enforced at six o'clock on the morning of Saturday July 17, 1948. Many Palestinian Jerusalemites, accepting the spirit of this truce, walked outside on Friday evening taking a breather from the fighting. With the truce becoming imminent, the Jewish forces planned a last-attempt attack to gain more territory. Their goal was to take both the Old City of Jerusalem and the Sheikh Jarrah neighborhood before the armistice. With time running out, they concentrated their attack on the Old City.

That night, my father's family was sitting at the front courtyard of Dar el-Adra, Home of the Virgin Monastery. Uncle Badie remembers the surprise attack began at about 9 p.m. that night. An estimated 1,600 shells, mostly mortar, fell on the Old City. One bomb fell in the monastery courtyard in front of my family and splashed shrapnel on them. Bassima, my grandma, and Ghada, my aunt, died instantly. Uncle Ibrahim lost his right arm. Shrapnel found its way into Aunt Bushra's right thigh. Basheer was hit in his stomach and his left knee. Bassim and Badie were protected by the wall that they were leaning against. Using the wall as cover, they began the gruesome task of carrying their mother's and sister's bodies inside and onto a bed. The rest of the family hid under beds while my father ran to ask for help at the emergency center of the Arab Red Cross. My mother, Suad, remembers hearing the noise of this shelling from Ramallah ten miles away. Mother was eleven years old. She followed her older brothers to the roof-top of their home and witnessed this bombardment. The sky over Jerusalem flashed with continuous yellow and orange light. The attack of the Old City lasted until three o'clock in the morning.

"Those days were marked by turmoil — a real big mess," my Uncle Badie recalls. 'Hundreds and thousands of Palestinians became homeless and refugees." Deir Yassin was not alone. My family's ordeal was not alone. Other villages were not alone. What happened in the spring of 1948 is incomprehensible. Ever since, it has become easy to dehumanize and reject the Palestinians. After all, they were refugees. Why build a memorial for refugees or for their dead?

The Memorial Landscape

There are no markers, no plaques, and no memorial to remind people of the massacre at Deir Yassin. By looking at Plate I, one can place Deir Yassin within the context of Jerusalem. This plate shows Jerusalem as defined by the United Nations partition plan of November 29, 1947. Plate II shows Deir Yassin's location today in relation to Yad Vashem. An aerial axis between these two sites is shown on this plate, reflecting the curious proximity of each site to the other. An appropriate location for a Palestinian memorial is on this axis at the southern end of Deir Yassin. This location connects the proposed memorial to its Arab and Palestinian roots, while at the same time extending it into a space that meets with the Jewish memorial. This memorial will be built to deserve respect, dignity, and sanctity, and to be modest and subdued, representing a solemn association with the dead and the great loss.

My idea for constructing a memorial landscape is simple but significant. It is based on an interplay between circles and squares. A large circle encompasses a square, and that in turn has a smaller circle within it. Even though these three elements are placed on one axis, that of Deir Yassin-Yad Vashem, their centers nevertheless do not converge into one. A close look at the site plan (Plate III) shows that the square center has shifted south away from Deir Yassin and towards Yad Vashem. The smaller circle inside the square has also shifted its center even further south. The imprint of this layout — a square and two circles — reflects an ancient architectural design. It was common for many old and traditional churches and mosques of the eastern Mediterranean to center a dome over a square with four columns at its corners.

In his book *Temples, Churches, and Mosques*, J. G. Davies discusses the evolution of the ancient Christian basilica with long naves into sixth century Byzantine churches built on the architectural principle of *baldachin*. *Baldachin* comes from the Italian word *baldacchino*, which in turn comes from *baldacco* in Baghdad, Iraq. *Baldacco* refers to a cloth canopy fixed or carried over an important person or a sacred object, or an ornamental structure resembling a canopy used over an altar. Hence, the evolution of an architectural principle based on a dome over a square anchored by four columns at the corners.

Islamic mosques evolved in a similar way to that of the Byzantine church, but for their own spiritual reasons. One of two types of mosque floor plans is the closed-plan mosque. This floor plan is based on a centralized and continuous space conducive to worship and again features a dome resting over four columns. The walls become non-structural but serve to create a space of worship. The Suleymaniye Mosque in Istanbul is a good example of such a floor plan.

This proposed memorial landscape design is an acknowledgment of the ancient tradition of *baldacchino*. Two circles, a square, and four columns pay tribute to the oldest and cherished traditions of the land. There are, however, two slight variations in this memorial landscape. The centers of the circles and square do not converge. As mentioned above, they shift slightly on the Deir Yassin-Yad Vashem axis. A second but more subtle variation is the absence of a dome or walls. Whereas ancient temples housed and protected their altars and worshipers, this temple has no building. It is a shrine naked to the sky. Plates VI and VII are conceptual drawings of the arrangement of this memorial landscape.

This arrangement creates a quiet and peaceful open space within the outer circle, while the square, depressed into the ground, becomes a reverend and somber space. The small circle, in turn, serves to create an eye, or a focal point for the memorial landscape — a location for a Palestinian monument. The larger circle has an enlarged arc that faces Yad Vashem stressing further the connection between both memorials. This reminds both Palestinians and Israelis of their connection. Palestinians and Israelis can no longer live assuming that the other does not exist.

Underneath the larger circle is a museum. Plate IV shows the floor plan of this museum, which has its entrance at the north edge of the square and its exit outside the outer circle. The two cross sections of Plate V show the relationship of the entrance and exit to the larger circle above. The museum layout serves to confuse its visitors by its maze-like arrangement. The exit is also difficult to find. As Palestinians and Israelis struggle to resolve their dispute, this museum will remind every visitor of the difficult task at hand. While looking for its exit, a visitor is again reminded of the commitment and perseverance of those toiling hard to find solutions.

There is a skylight built into this memorial landscape. The skylight is a thin and long strip of glass laid into the ground of the larger circle. It extends from the main gate of the site to the northern edge of the depressed square. This skylight serves both to shed light into the museum below and to draw visitors towards the square as they first enter. The skylight is placed on the Deir Yassin-Yad Vashem axis and is one of two features that a visitor initially sees. The other feature is the presence of four columns at the corners of the depressed square inside the larger circle. These columns are not round and tall, but square, wide, and short representing the heavy burden of injustice that Palestinians carry with them. These columns would support a dome if it ever existed.

This memorial landscape also features amphitheater-like steps to be used for outside lectures, group discussions, or ceremonies. These steps are located in two places: around the depressed square facing the eye or focal point, and at the southern arc of the larger circle facing north. Both sets of steps are to be simple and subdued, to create no interfere with the sanctity created by the memorial landscape.

Like most buildings in the eastern Mediterranean, this structure will be built from stone. Stone symbolizes many things, particularly in Palestine. It reminds Palestinians of the rootedness to their land. It is part of the centuries-old heritage left undisturbed through the ancient and beautiful buildings of Palestine. Stone helped preserve these buildings and the heritage they carry. Stone also reminds many of the Palestinian uprising, the Intifada, its crushed bones and spilled blood. Still, stone is what tourists to the Holy Land come to see from the outside world, often forgetting to visit with the people of Palestine. People who were entrusted with the land and, like stone, preserved its heritage for centuries. These same people became the living stones while stone itself became the silent competitor, robbing the connection between the living stones of the land and tourists from the outside world.

It is most fitting that the living stones of Palestine construct this memorial and its landscape using stone — the silent stone. With this, they would both commemorate their dark history, but also symbolize a turning point and a different future. Construction would symbolize the livelihood and presence of the living stones. As equal partners in their land, Palestinians would be free to construct this memorial and its landscape. This turning point will witness a new era of two peoples committed to one brighter future.

With its completion, the silent stones of this memorial and landscape will no longer compete with the living stones. Rather, they will become a sign of the presence of the living stones and a vehicle for them to reconnect with the outside world. Holy Land visitors must not complete their tour without visiting Deir Yassin and experiencing the village, landscape, and memorial, and learning the message the site carries.

Building this memorial will be a process that heals wounds and builds trust. Healing and trusting become a prelude to complete forgiveness. Palestinian and Israeli children can meet at the site and witness its construction. Togetherness becomes valuable for these children. Israeli children can learn about the bloody past of their fathers, while Palestinian children can better understand how their parents were dehumanized and why they carry a wounded spirit. Both children can learn why their parents avoid talking about the real details of their past.

By the time readers hold and read this book, fifty years would have passed since the catastrophic year of 1948. Palestinians endured fifty harsh years with no resolution to their suffering in sight. This fiftieth year commemoration can be the beginning of a different relationship between both peoples; one marked by their acceptance of the necessity of building a Palestinian memorial and by the implementation of the construction of such a memorial.

While visiting this sacred ground, people can see the silent stones and visit the living dead. Like a mausoleum, the museum gives visitors the opportunity to walk through its hallways, feel Palestinian pain, and share their grief. Visitors will then climb up the exit stairs and walk into daylight, a symbol of a new beginning — a rebirth. This exit will not be at the sacred ground, but close to or maybe within the Deir Yassin buildings, symbolizing the Palestinian connection to their past.

With the two hills in such close proximity, visiting Yad Vashem without acknowledging what happened to the Palestinian people is an incomplete experience. In the same manner, visiting a Palestinian memorial at Deir Yassin without acknowledging the history of the Jewish people is also an incomplete experience. It is with this irony that the Jewish memorial and a new Palestinian memorial would connect. As this proximity is ironic, its awareness becomes essential. Should a Yad Vashem visitor receive a Deir Yassin pamphlet? Would mounting a Deir Yassin plaque at the northern end of Yad Vashem make this connection? Or should tour-guides simply take their groups to visit Deir Yassin?

If all the sketches are clear (plates I through V), one can turn to the conceptual drawings (plates VI and VII), to follow the intended experience of the proposed Deir Yassin memorial landscape. As visitors first enter the memorial ground, they can only see the four square columns in front of them and the skylight strip leading them forward. Extending their view, visitors will also see at a distance the building of Yad Vashem. The four Palestinian columns frame the distant Jewish memorial. One is forced to contemplate the Jewish history in Europe while at the same time thinking "how about the Palestinians?" This is a common theme that is often echoed by Palestinians who see themselves as

having to suffer the consequences of events that have taken place in
Europe far from their land. Such fear will gradually dissipate as one
walks forward on this sacred ground. The tilted flat surface of the square
begins to reveal itself, with the memorial focal point competing for attention with Yad Vashem. As visitors reach the end of the skylight
strip, they are stopped by the northern edge of the square. That point
overlooks both the Jewish Holocaust memorial at a distance and the
Palestinian massacre memorial in the foreground — a point where they
must stop.

This is a point in time and place for reflection. While Yad Vashem
sits on the highest hilltop overlooking its surroundings, the Palestinian memorial is subdued and impressed into the ground. While Yad
Vashem covers its victims, the Deir Yassin memorial is left with foot-
prints but no building. This is a time for reflection on the absence of
sanctity. Deir Yassin is a place were human brutality was left un-
checked, where one victimized people turned oppressor and another
was subdued into a state of near extinction. The eye or focal point of
the Palestinian memorial landscape faces the viewer with its back to
the Jewish Holocaust memorial, as though a victim pleading for help
and empathy, while running away from its oppressor.

The memorial offers a point in time and place were one can contemplate cruelty in history. Again, with both memorials in sight, the layout becomes conducive to reflection. As one is pulled forward by the
skylight strip, the northern edge of the square abruptly halts such
movement. This is not unlike the events of 1948 in Palestine — a harsh
and abrupt shift in the natural flow of life. Palestinians can look at
both memorials and become aware of the deep connection of European
history to their own suffering. Jews can also visit this memorial and,
like Palestinians, look at both memorials and recognize how their history in Europe affected their attitude towards and their treatment of
the Palestinians.

To continue, a visitor has to go around the columns, walk further
south, and join the Palestinian memorial by turning away from Yad
Vashem and looking forward and down at the entrance to the
memorial museum. This is another point in time and space that has
significance. Turning away from Yad Vashem signifies a visitor's
willingness to concentrate on and embrace Palestinian history and
the Palestinian plight without distractions. A visitor now descends
into the ground, surrounded by walls that increasingly separate one
from the outside world. This descent becomes about experiencing
togetherness with Palestinians and a oneness with the memorial.
Above the entrance one finds a large surface of glass with etchings
of names of all the Palestinian villages destroyed during 1947 and
after. Until this point, the memorial does not share any names with
its visitors, leaving them to relate to their surroundings by simply

being at the site and feeling its sanctity and the message it holds.

Many people may not clearly see those faint village names etched into the glass just above eye-level. "Yes, we know," one might think. But do they really know? People often talk about the Palestinian tragedy, but very few know or can relate to its magnitude. Even Palestinians who personally suffered, are astounded when they learn the details of their own people's experience. Behind all the names and numbers that one sees, the humanness of this suffering can be revealed. Villages, orchards, homes, families, mothers, and children were all afflicted. Many people do not know.

As soon as one enters the museum itself, one is faced with a large blank wall that captures the shadow of these village names. Village names are directly before your eyes. They are names in your face. Names that you used to know but have forgotten, and others that you used to visit but now cannot. All these are village names right in front of you. You realize that now you know what you did not know. By now it is also too late. Unlike an etching on a wall or glass that one can feel, these villages have become shadows. Reach out and touch, but you cannot feel.

This would be a fascinating experience for children. Children would see and read the shadows of the 443 village names on each others' faces and hands. Adults, especially those coming from lost villages, would also stand in that spot and see the name of their own village on their bodies. They would gasp with astonishment.

Moving further, a visitor walks around this wall and descends once more into the ground. The mood shifts dramatically. Until this point, one was connected to the outside world and its natural daylight, but now a visitor enters a dark realm marked with black and gray. Natural daylight begins to fade as one walks into the museum. The only light in this area comes from the skylight strip built on the Yad Vashem-Deir Yassin axis into the roof, the floor of the outside larger circle. In the museum one learns about the horrific details of the massacre, looks at tangible reminders, and reads the names of the dead. The silent stones, now seen from inside the museum as both structure and part of the exhibit, remind visitors once again of the presence and livelihood of the living stones — people who work tirelessly to give this site back its name.

As visitors find the exit and proceed to leave, they must climb a set of stairs that become increasingly steep. The exit area also narrows as one ascends to the outside. Palestinian village names are once again etched into these walls. You can reach out and touch, and this time feel the words, connect, and not forget. Natural light will allow these names to become more pronounced as one moves up the stairs. The last two or three steps would require slightly more effort than that of a regular big step as a symbol of the struggle victims go through to come back to life, to heal, and to stand on equal ground within the human family. The location of this exit is outside the larger circle of the memorial landscape, close to or among the village buildings.

What Will Happen to Deir Yassin?

Why build a memorial for refugees or for their dead? With the above discussion in mind, stones used to build this memorial landscape will take on a whole new meaning. As part of this new context, these silent stones are configured not to compete with, but to represent the presence of the living stones. The memorial location, coupled with the absence of a protective dome, signifies the human capacity for savagery as well as our own helplessness in its face. A memorial at the massacre site is a physical reminder of this ultimate failure, and the deep suffering that it has caused.

Visiting Deir Yassin and the massacre memorial would undoubtedly be a painful experience for Palestinians. Still, it is crucial that they be there and feel the agony of their past. With that, they can bring life back to Deir Yassin and its forgotten history. This history will now be among Palestinians and for Palestinians. Palestinians can simultaneously memorialize and celebrate a site that once brought on them a cruel incident that threw them into despair, but now hosts a memorial that serves to bring back life and hope. Such a dynamic serves to bring Palestinians to terms with their history while at the same time giving them the courage to move forward with their future.

While working on this project, I could not help but think to myself, "How about Deir Yassin?" What about all the buildings with walls, rooms, and gardens? These buildings hold many dear memories, not only those of the massacre. Memories of children playing, mothers tending to their chores, and fathers working — memories of a song and a smile. These are memories taken away from Deir Yassin's original inhabitants. What should be done to this village?

Palestinians lost entire towns and villages. Israelis either inhabit Palestinian towns and villages and have completely altered their character, or they have demolished them. My Uncle Basheer, who almost died from bomb shrapnel in his stomach, lived on to document Israel's destruction of 443 Palestinian villages. His book, *Towards the De-Arabization of Palestine/Israel, 1945-1977*, tells the other side of a story that many do not hear.

Palestinians who cannot go back to visit their villages can instead visit Deir Yassin and reminisce about their past. Deir Yassin can become a symbol of towns lost and dreams stolen. For this, the village of Deir Yassin must be preserved as an historic Palestinian site, and its buildings converted into a campus to host a Palestinian institution, like a school of history, a conservatory of cultural studies, or established organizations like al-Haq, a Palestinian human rights organization, or Sabeel, a Palestinian Christian liberation movement.

The conditions that Palestinians are living under have dramatically worsened today. Since the catastrophe happened, fifty years have passed with no resolution to the Palestinian suffering. The Oslo Accord, with both its ambitious vision and its shortcomings, has not yet produced a situation of mutual respect and trust, nor has it resolved the many tangled and pressing issues. Palestinians are still being victimized and living as prisoners in their own country or as strangers in the diaspora. Israelis, like jailers on duty, are restrained in their role as oppressors. Nevertheless, the Oslo Accord is a route taken by the leaders of both peoples. Like visitors walking in the memorial museum, both peoples must toil through confusing and often dark walkways of the accord to inch towards a mutual respect that comes only through both peoples having equal rights and equal freedoms in a land both claim and cherish.

One day might come when Palestinian and Israeli children, living together as equals, will visit both Deir Yassin and Yad Vashem and look back at history with astonishment. "How could our ancestors do this? Didn't they know that they all belonged to this one land?" When that day comes, Palestinian children can invite Israeli children to hold a joint prayer at the Deir Yassin memorial, close off the museum, and move its exhibition to the buildings of the village of Deir Yassin. That celebration will become a symbol of reconciliation and closure. The joint prayer will become a mark of forgiveness that a Palestinian memorial will carry with it. Palestinians and Israelis — Christians, Muslims, and Jews — living together as equals, will rejoice for bringing reverence back to the Holy Land. Naim Ateek, in his book *Justice and Only Justice* writes: "The land can, however, become holy to those who put their trust in the God of the whole universe, whose nature does not change — a God of justice for all, who desires goodness and mercy for all people living in this and every land."

PLATES

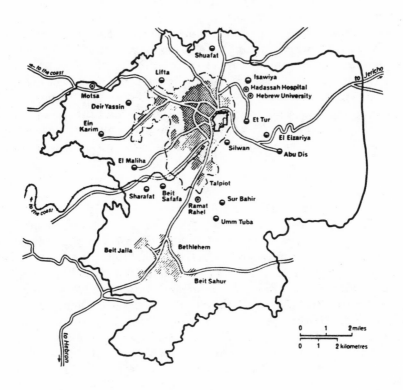

Plate I. Jerusalem - United Nations Partition Plan
29 November, 1947

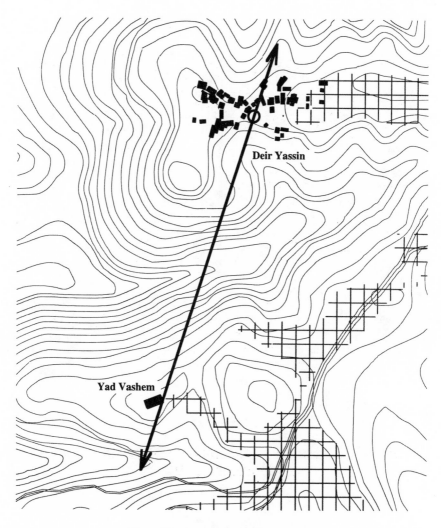

Plate II. Aerial Axis Connecting
Deir Yassin with Yad Vashem

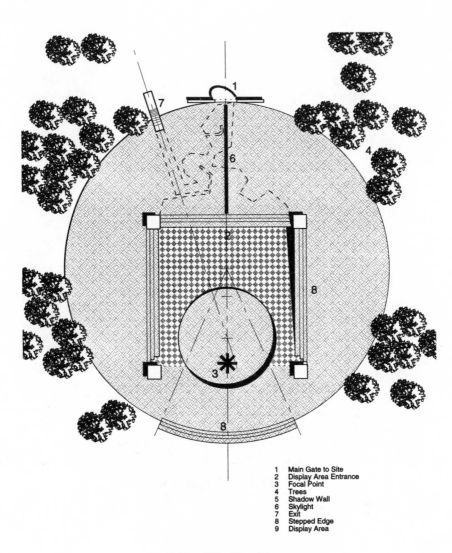

1   Main Gate to Site
2   Display Area Entrance
3   Focal Point
4   Trees
5   Shadow Wall
6   Skylight
7   Exit
8   Stepped Edge
9   Display Area

Plate III. Site Plan

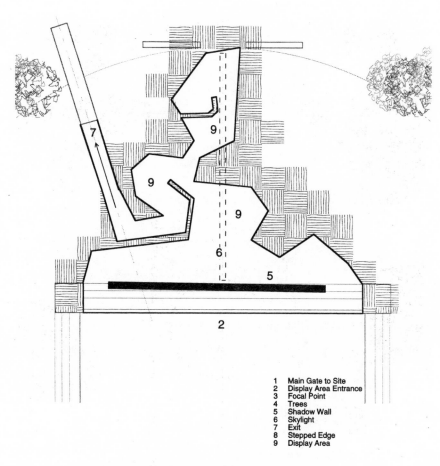

1 Main Gate to Site
2 Display Area Entrance
3 Focal Point
4 Trees
5 Shadow Wall
6 Skylight
7 Exit
8 Stepped Edge
9 Display Area

Plate IV. Display Area

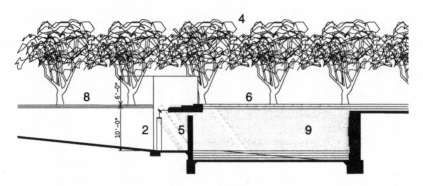

Section through Entrance to Display Area

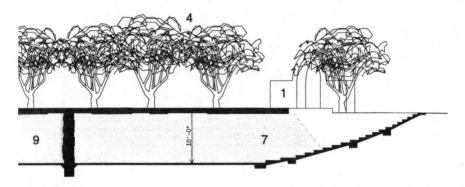

Section through Exit from Display Area

1   Main Gate to Site
2   Display Area Entrance
3   Focal Point
4   Trees
5   Shadow Wall
6   Skylight
7   Exit
8   Stepped Edge
9   Display Area

Plate V. Cross Sections

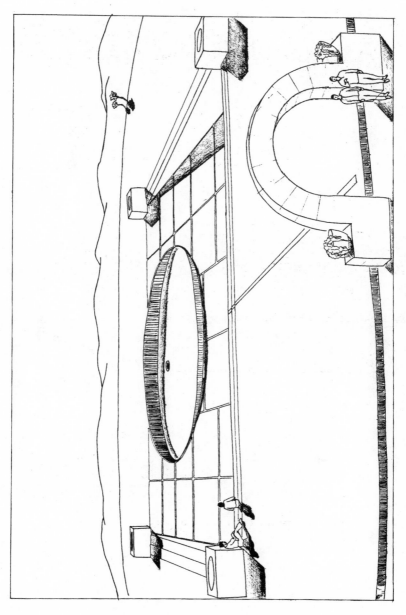

Plate VI. Conceptual Drawing - Eye Level

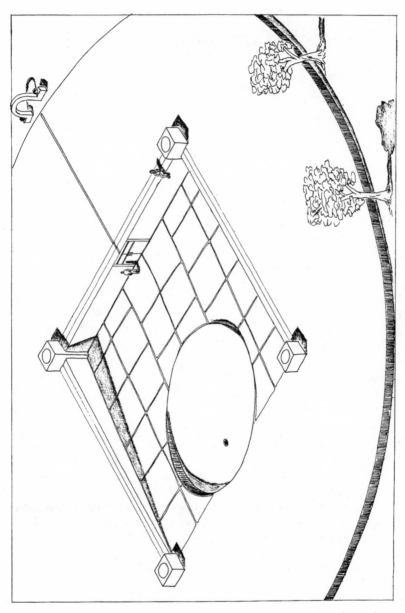

Plate VII. Conceptual Drawing - Bird's Eye View

8

The Last Memorials to Atrocity in the Holy Land?

by Rami G. Khouri

Much of the complexity of conflict resolution in the Middle East, especially in the Arab-Israeli sector, is about vanquishing the injustices, atrocities, and pains of the past. In April 1997, a gathering in the town of Bireh in Palestine provided an opportunity for Arabs and Israelis to grapple with this vexed burden of painful national memory and responsibility, and it also highlighted the role of forgiveness and reconciliation in conflict resolution.

The Bireh gathering of Christians, Muslims, and Jews from this region and from other countries took place in the form of a conference to commemorate the 49th anniversary of the massacre at Deir Yassin, a village west of Jerusalem where Jewish commandos killed over 100 Palestinians, mostly in cold blood. The Bireh conference was one component of the Deir Yassin Remembered project, which was launched in 1995 by the activism of an American university professor named Daniel McGowan. It aims to raise $100,000 to erect a permanent memorial at the site of the former village of Deir Yassin, now located in Israel, west of Jerusalem. Ironically, perhaps appropriately, and certainly controversially for many, the proposed Deir Yassin memorial would stand north and within sight of Yad Vashem, Israel's powerful Holocaust monument, memorial, and museum.

Time has only accentuated the brutal vulgarity of what happened at Deir Yassin. On April 9, 1948, several weeks before the end of the British mandate in Palestine, Jewish commandos from the Irgun and Stern Gang attacked the village of Deir Yassin and killed over 100 people, half of them women and children. Twenty-five Palestinian men were loaded into trucks, paraded through a section of Jerusalem, and then shot in cold blood in a quarry. When the operation was over, many Palestinian Arabs at Deir Yassin had been killed, and the rest of the 750 villagers fled to Jerusalem. Within hours, as word of the attack spread throughout Palestine, frightened Palestinians as far away as Haifa fled their homes in fear of meeting a similar fate.

The panic and mass Arab flight sparked by the Jewish attack on Deir Yassin — ethnic cleansing of the first order — achieved its goals. In the subsequent weeks and months, the integrity of traditional Palestine collapsed. Over 400 Palestinian villages disappeared off the face of the map. Hundreds of thousands of Palestinians became refugees. The state of Israel came into being. The wholeness and reconstitution of Jewish national life in Israel coincided with the fragmentation and dispersal of the Palestinian community. Deir Yassin, for Arabs, remains the most profound symbol of this momentous historical phenomenon — the simultaneous birth of Israel, and the fatal wounding of Palestine.

A monument to Deir Yassin would merely manifest in physical terms that which is already permanently etched into the Palestinian and Arab psyche — enduring remembrance of Arab vulnerability and weakness at a certain time and place, a particular moment in history and geography when Arab community and humanity vanished instantly before the knives and bullets of a determined Jewish death squad. Deir Yassin still haunts us because it still dehumanizes us in two dimensions: it recalls the agony of past helplessness, and it also warns of weakness, denial and vulnerability as the recurring nightmare of our possibly perpetual dehumanization. For what is there to prevent us again from being paraded in trucks, shot in cold blood in quarries, and buried in mass graves in the lands of our ancestors — as has recently happened in central Europe, land of the Enlightenment, democracy, and liberalism, where dehumanization was further redefined this decade through the use of mass rape as an instrument of deliberate cruelty.

Like all atrocities, Deir Yassin left behind multiple victims — the dead and the living, the targets of the violence and also its perpetrators. A monument at Deir Yassin, within eyesight of Yad Vashem, could unlock powerful forces of truthfulness among Arabs and Israelis alike. It could permit both peoples, separately or together, to vanquish the pains of the past by ending the tendency by both sides to refuse to acknowledge the suffering and dehumanization that each experienced in their own history. Most Arabs today tend to deny the totality of Jewish historical suffering primarily because most Israelis will not explicitly acknowledge Jewish responsibility for the violence that Jews and Israelis have used against Palestinians. Mutual denial and historical deception have not served these peoples well.

A memorial at Deir Yassin could transform the current cycle of mutual denial into a more morally responsible and historically constructive cycle of acknowledgment of the past, understanding, compassion, and, ultimately, forgiveness and reconciliation. It would help to heal the still open and festering Palestinian wound that comes from the feeling that Palestinians do not exist, that their villages can be erased from the face of the earth by the hundreds, that their men can be paraded in trucks, and slaughtered in quarries. More than any other political gesture, a memorial to Deir Yassin would be an act of moral compensation that would allow Palestinians to see themselves, and Israelis, in a different, more constructive, way. For, just as Deir Yassin is visible from Yad Vashem, so is Yad Vashem visible from Deir Yassin. Only Palestinians and Arabs whose humanity has been returned to them can truly see Yad Vashem — not just see it physically, but absorb its enormous moral and historical meaning, which most Arabs refuse to do as a conscious political act.

Jewish and Palestinian historical suffering are separated by many dimensions of time, place, scale, and consequence, but they are united by a single fact: they can only be fully overcome by a process of rehumanization that acknowledges the brutality and criminality of past deeds. That process has been underway for many years for Jews and Israelis, and it will continue for many more, as it should. A parallel process has not yet started, though, between Israelis and Palestinians. The importance of a memorial to Deir Yassin is not just that it could spark an Israeli rehumanization of Palestinians; equally important, it could also spark a simultaneous Palestinian rehumanization of Israelis.

Last year, the Centre for the Study of Forgiveness and Reconciliation was inaugurated at Coventry University in England. It arose from a realization that forgiveness and reconciliation raise two distinct but related issues with global consequences: "One, the fact that people need to take responsibility for their actions, and, two, the importance of remorse, apology, forgiveness, and reconciliation as vital elements in peacemaking, and peace-keeping.... It is becoming clearer than ever that public apologies leading to a healing process and forgiveness... reaffirm the humanity of people often denied or brutalized during past conflict. In the long run, accepting responsibility for one's actions in the past, and expressing remorse and regret, may prove to be the most important elements in the process of healing and a prime condition for genuine peace and stability worldwide."

Deir Yassin was the site of a massacre; Yad Vashem recalls the evil of genocide. The awkward line of sight between the two suggests an opportunity for both Israelis and Palestinians finally to get beyond the agonies of their past vulnerabilities. May these be the last memorials to atrocity in the Holy Land?

PART TWO

The Future of Israel/Palestine

9

On the New Diaspora: A Jewish Meditation on the Future of Israel/Palestine

by Marc H. Ellis

For those of us who live in America and have been working for justice in the Middle East, the time of reckoning has come. Or rather, the time may already have passed. Perhaps we have been fooling ourselves over the years thinking that the complicated process for peace in the Middle East would be resolved in an efficacious and just way.

The agenda for Americans seeking peace and justice in the Middle East has been diverse and in some ways misleading. In the many conferences, bulletins, journals, and books, in the small groups that have come and gone over the years, the case has been made for justice, especially with regard to the struggle in Israel and Palestine, but mostly in theory, in abstractions that bear little relation to the facts on the ground. Veterans in the struggle surely recognize that every glimpse of hope over the last years has been in the context of diminishing land and prospects for justice. The Oslo accords demonstrate this fact in a dramatic way: as the possibility of a new relationship between Jew and Palestinian in the Middle East came to fruition, the map of Oslo signaled a victory for Israel that dwarfed previous scenarios of a final settlement. Since the celebration of the Oslo signing, a further gap between Jew and Palestinian has arisen. The enclosing ring of Jewish settlements around Jerusalem, signified by the buildings on the hills of Har Homa/Abu Ghneim, simply solidifies the sense of a permanent and unequal distribution of land and resources in Israel/Palestine.

What is it that went wrong? How did those who struggle find themselves in the place of celebrating events which when scrutinized closely and objectively can be seen as disasters and defeats?

We can begin the critique in many places: an inaccurate political analysis of American foreign policy; underestimation of the strength of Israel and the weakness of the Arab world; refusal to address the failure of the Palestinian leadership and diaspora; inability of progressive secular and Christian movements to address boldly the essence of the geopolitical questions in the Middle East; miscalculating the strength of the Jewish lobby in the West and the failure of Jewish liberals to speak boldly and consistently. If we take each analysis and constituency by itself, the factors for failure are diverse and complex. When taken together, the possibility of a just peace between Israel and Palestine seems inconceivable. It is almost as if the Palestinians were, at least for this century, on the other side of history, with external and internal forces either too weak or arrayed against them. In this way the Palestinians take on a place in history not dissimilar to the place of the Jews in Europe during the 1930s. Despite the retrospective analysis and accusations, once the policies of the Nazis were in place, the Jewish community in Europe was doomed. So, too, with the Palestinians. Once the state of Israel was founded, the situation of the Palestinians deteriorated from that time until today. Rather than a series of exceptional policies, wars, and circumstances, the displacement of the Palestinians and the expropriation of their land have followed a straight and logical course. And this despite Palestinian protest, internal Jewish dissent, and increasing numbers of people around the world who have mobilized in defense of the Palestinian people.

Still, within the overall framework of defeat, the struggle for justice and peace in the Middle East has been important on a variety of levels, not the least of which is a rising and sustainable public voice for accountability for the plight of the Palestinians. On the practical level, the success of the protest movement has been to limit the advance of Israel and thus help stay or at least minimize the defeat of the Palestinians. By providing a public space for dissent, those in the struggle have forced those who legitimize the scenario of Jewish victory/Palestinian defeat at times to hold back or at least admit some culpability in the displacement of the Palestinian people. In doing so, time has been bought — some time is even now left — to redress the unequal situation if the will to do so is found. Buying time in a situation such as this is valuable on many levels, not the least of which is the interval for adversaries in the conflict to search through the values they espouse and embody. In terms of Jewish history, for example, contrasting the value of justice spoken of by Jews with the injustice of Israeli policies can have the effect, perhaps delayed, of opening the Jewish tradition to move beyond its sense of innocence. In terms of Palestinian history, time has allowed the articulation of Palestinian aspirations on the international scene.

Within the context of Jewish history, the failure to address the displacement of Palestinians has had catastrophic consequences. The long struggle for Jews to survive as a people and derive from their tradition a matrix of sensibilities and values is noteworthy; that its epiphany was reached in the aftermath of the most difficult, if not impossible of circumstances — the mass slaughter of European Jews — borders on the miraculous. That at this same moment a segment of world Jewry, with the acquiescence and later almost total support of Jewish leadership in Europe and North America, would embark on the enterprise of state building that required the dislocation of another people is unfortunate, though perhaps understandable within the context of the Holocaust. What is unforgivable, though, is the continuous expansion of the state after the 1967 war, the brutal invasion of Lebanon, the policy of might and beatings in response to the Palestinian intifada, and the details of the Oslo accords that enshrine the victory of Israel and defeat for Palestinians. What is even more unforgivable is the continuation of these policies after the Palestinian surrender at Oslo. In the era of Netanyahu the cost of the Palestinian surrender escalates, as if the surrender itself allows a new round of expropriation, dislocation, and settlements, as if the historical emergency after the Holocaust has issued decades later into a desire to humiliate a vanquished foe.

A surrender is sometimes necessary in history to insure the survival of a people. At the same time it represents an appeal to the victor to reconcile as far as possible the claims of both parties. Though it seems to be contradictory, surrender also involves an appeal to the moral values of the victor. It is a condition of complete vulnerability. Will the victor recognize this vulnerability, see it in its own historical journey, and thus seek to minimize the humiliation of the defeated? The appeal to moral values in the victor is also an appeal to end a cycle of struggle and death which precipitated the initial conflict. Will the cycle of death and destruction end when the victor leaves the defeated only with the desire to regain enough strength to defeat and humiliate those who dominate? Surrender may thus be a strategic option as well as a moral appeal — yet both of these elements seems to have fallen on the deaf ears of a victorious Israel.

We might say, since many Israelis have ambivalent feelings about the present direction of the government, that Israel as a nation-state is rebuffing the strategic and moral appeals of the Palestinians. Nation-states hardly recognize vulnerability except out of a perceived interest, and when that vulnerability allows the state to advance its policies and cover them with a veneer of charity and innocence. The rhetoric of the state acknowledges the surrender and pretends that the acceptance of the surrender is done within a moral framework. Rarely does a nation-state acknowledge the ambiguities of history and in its victory also acknowledge it own complicity in the conflict. In short, nation-states are long on self-congratulatory epistles but short on heart-felt confessions. In this way, Israel makes its claim as a nation among other nations. Power makes right and there are always those in the intellectual and religious community who will articulate and legitimize the victory in the language of the state.

Marginalizing Dissent

Yet the problem runs deeper than the inability of Israel to hear the strategic and moral plight of the Palestinians. Rather it extends to the inability of Israel to hear and respond to Jewish strategic and moral dissent over its policies. This is part of the difficulty that Jewish dissenters have had and for which they were unprepared. The Jewish state emerges from a history characterized by suffering. This suffering has been judged unwarranted and a violation of Jewish life and values. At least from the vantage point of suffering, the state emerges as a vehicle of Jewish survival and as a framework that helps to carry on the life and values of the people. It is the very violation of these values in Europe which necessitates the creation of the state, and the state as heir to Jewish history takes upon itself the claim to continue that which was so recently threatened with annihilation. Israel is so founded and the text of its declaration of statehood is filled with these allusions and claims. Moreover, the claim is cast much wider than for the citizens found within its borders, or one might say — since the state is primarily for all its Jewish citizens rather than the Palestinian Arabs left within the newly defined borders — that Israel is founded for all Jews everywhere as the guarantor of the continuation of Jewish history.

Early on in the development of Israel, the voices of dissent to the establishment of the state and those who, though in favor of the state, dissented from some of its fundamental policies were placed on the periphery of state discourse or dismissed as enemies. The penalty for such dissent was marginalization or excommunication from the Jewish community. Over time, dissent itself tended to be seen as something outside the possibilities of Jewish discourse and hence outside the Jewish community. This tendency continues today even after the power of Israel and its place among the nations is secure. The claim in representing Jewish history and continuity takes on the aspect of a total and unreflective commitment, even as the state narrows the definition of who is and who is not a Jew.

Thus Israel, like any state, seeks victory in its fight to survive and expand and dismisses its dissenters as those to be ignored or exiled from acceptable discourse. At the same time, Israel seeks a redefinition of the content and practice of Judaism and Jewish life. Suffering is to be overcome through the vehicle of the state, but so too is the tendency to emphasize certain values of justice deeply ingrained in the history of the Jewish people. Jewish dissenters are thus caught in a bind which even today most do not realize: emphasizing the values of justice and compassion to build an empowered Jewish presence in the world, most particularly in the Middle East, as Israel itself is systematically violating these values with regard to the Palestinian people. The state carries that rhetoric, in fact fuels its narrative at home and abroad and within that framework elicits support around the world, as Jewish liberals hone its vocabulary, write its history, and carry its message to the universities and the broader public, especially in the West. When state policy is clearly in violation of these values, most Jewish liberals continue the cause with particular criticisms and over-all support of Israel, at the same time participating in the silencing of those who question the overall framework of the state and its policies. Historically, Jewish dissent increasingly has been voiced for a state whose policies it cannot support but whose overall existence needs to be defended against all comers. The "existence" issue becomes so domi-nant that defense of the state is judged more important than the ethi-cal issues at hand or, more to the point, the ethical issues are only to be argued within this overall framework. All nation-states thrive on the rhetoric of dissenters who argue the overall project of the state as inno-cent and redemptive while criticizing particular policies which to their mind are secondary to the project itself. Israel, carrying with it a pecu-liar history of suffering, dispersion, and ingathering, has lived on this kind of dissent as a proof of the larger intent of Jews while protecting the power of the state to carry on with its policies of expansion and displacement.

Perhaps the protection of the state by liberals who limit forms of dissent was inevitable given both the long history of the Jewish people and recent events. Though powerful within the context of the Middle East, Israel nevertheless was and continues to be vulnerable. As a small state beholden to western military and economic support, and with a narrative of suffering and redemption to orient that support, the possibility that building the state is both important to Jews *and* a disaster to Palestinians is too difficult to articulate in a framework that elicits unwavering support for Israel. As the accusations against Israeli policies escalated in the 1980s and 1990s, and the horror of some of these policies could no longer be denied, the threat posed by the possible indictment of Jews increased outside the state as well. That is, the narrative of the founding and empowerment of Israel as a compensatory event for the Holocaust and as an example of a pioneering, creative effort to reclaim the desert for cultivation and consumption — a narrative that bode well for Jews in the West — threatened to unravel. In fact, the status of Jews outside the state was buoyed in the 1950s and 1960s by the accomplishments of Israel, proving to others that Jews were capable of self-government and could succeed against great odds. The heroic saga of Israel became emblematic of the heroic saga of Jews in general. Jews outside Israel took as much or more pride in the success of the state and identified with it, often times more uncritically than Jews within Israel. In turn Jews became identified with the state by non-Jews. Of course, the good, surviving, creative, and empowered Jew could easily become — one might say revert — to the Jewish stereotypes of previous ages, with predictable results. In this sense, the protection of Israel by Jewish liberals who would have criticized without restraint similar policies by another state, including the United States where many of these liberals live, became a protection of Jewish status in the West. Speaking good of Israel or at least limiting dissent on its policies became for most Jewish intellectuals a domestic policy. Palestinians were largely absent from this discussion even as they were talked about endlessly; so too were Israelis, who again were talked about endlessly and were at the same time absent from the discussion. In the end, the discussion about Israel in the West is not about Israel at all. Rather it is about Jewish history in Europe and Jewish ascendancy in North America; ironically, the same history which had given rise to Israel in the first place and has supported it so vigorously since its founding.

And so it remains today after Oslo. The Oslo accords reversed the difficult period of adjustment for Jews in the West. The invasion of Lebanon and the violent response to the Palestinian intifada carried images of Jews which are contrary to the image that Jews have of themselves and want others to have of them. The signing of the accords on the White House lawn in 1993 signified to the larger public the end of the struggle in Israel and Palestine and a just outcome to a conflict which seemed intractable. Blessed by the president of the United States, with oratory from Prime Minister Rabin that affirmed the Biblical promise of justice and compassion, the occasion seemed to put to rest the accusing images of past decades. The Jewish community, most notably Jewish liberals, welcomed the "end" of the conflict as a vindication of their position that Israel, despite minor lapses, is good and just. With the Palestinians recognized and Israel secure, the front page headlines involving Israel and the conflict within the Jewish community over Israeli policies was now over. The narrative of suffering and redemption, though tarnished, could be raised to a level of permanence within the West. Israel secure — and, as importantly, out of the news — meant Jewish life and status in the West is also secure.

The Last Exile

This complicated scenario within the Jewish world featuring those who criticize Israel as its primary defenders cannot exist and flourish without Christians who feel a need to defend Israel because of the history of Jewish suffering in Europe. The Christian understanding of Jews and Israel is complicated, instructed by more than a millennium of Christian anti-Jewishness as well as interpretations of the Bible that see Jews as central to Christian witness and life. Both the liberal and conservative segments of the Christian community are drawn into the drama of Israel by way of history and scripture. The historical saga of anti-Jewishness elicits a confessional strain of Christianity and thus support for a state where Jews can be free after so much suffering, the scriptural focus promoting a sense of the Jewish return to the Holy Land as a precursor to the return of the messiah and the inauguration of the messianic age. What is important in both these understandings is that, as with the Jewish debate in the West, both are domestic affairs, relating to European history and to Christianity. The Palestinians are essentially absent, or if present act as foils for the larger Jewish and Christian drama: the Jewish drama is in the foreground but only as it relates to the more significant Christian drama of confession and salvation. As since the beginning of Christianity, the Jews are at the center *and* at the same time are peripheral. The Jews represent the struggle of Christians to define or redefine their own tradition, history, and teleology.

In this process the ecumenical dialogue, promoted by liberal Christians after the Holocaust, turns into a "deal" whereby Jews demand Jewish self-identification as well as the confession of Christian sins, while Christians are limited to that self-identification and confession. Since both identity and confession involve the support of Israel by Christians, renunciation of the ability to criticize Israel, or even interact critically with Judaism and Jewish life at any level, the deal is sealed with a pledge of silence. Once Jews criticize Israel then Christians can nod in assent but any independent movement of criticism is seen as reneging on the demands that Christians have acceded to. Criticism of Israel outside the parameters of Jewish dissent is seen as retreating to the anti-Jewish position of yesteryear. The reality of anti-Jewishness is seen now primarily in terms of wavering support of Christians for Israel and thus a permanent danger to be monitored by the Jewish community. The penalty of being labeled anti-Jewish is constantly brandished.

There have been Jews and Christians who have struggled against these parameters set by the Jewish community within the ecumenical deal, but by and large they have struggled without institutional and communal support. To speak openly and boldly carries with it the prospect of exile, a cost that few are willing to bear. When the risk is taken, there are few bases of support upon which to rely. Jews who speak against the consensus, especially against the liberal consensus, are immediately exiled, and the Christian constituency that supports such dissent and which uses that dissent to gain "permission" to speak from their own perspective has an agenda that includes Jews and Israel but does not focus exclusively on these issues. These Christians are in a fight with their own tradition and community — in a Christian exile if you will — and while celebrating Jewish prophetic speech and action are often unwilling to do more than verbally support such efforts. In one sense there is a parallel of exiles between these Jews and Christians, though with a fundamental proviso: the community of Christians being substantially more numerous yields a much larger dissenting community and this community has a more diverse focus. Jewish dissenters therefore have few places to go for support and the pressure exerted by the Jewish community to silence dissent makes the costs for Christians higher than most are willing to bear. Jews in exile are truly alone.

Nonetheless the responsibility for the failure of Jewish dissent must ultimately be borne by Jews themselves. In the end, Jews could not anticipate an empowered state that radically changed the stakes of Jewish history. In essence the state of Israel, acting like any other state, must be analyzed and confronted in those terms rather than from a Jewish moral and ethical framework. That latter is either used to obfuscate the issue or, because of the power of the state, is inadequate to the task at hand. Either way Jewish dissent couched in this language is unable to prevent Israel from its continuing — and, from the perspective of the nation-state system, logical — unfolding in the complete destruction of Palestine. At the same time and in the larger framework of Jewish history, the collapse of the moral and ethical framework means the end of Judaism and Jewish life as we know it and the recreation of an exilic reality without the foundations which guided such exiles in the past. Paradoxically, this exile is made up of Jews driven from the community because of this moral and ethical framework which they inherited and which is now atrophying in their lifetime. Because this framework continues to be articulated by the state and those who legitimate state policies — that is by those systematically violating this framework — even its simple articulation becomes hypocritical. This exilic community, perhaps the last in Jewish history, is one that finds the language of the tradition unspeakable.

After the Holocaust and the state of Israel, it is at this place that Jews have arrived. Where can such an exile lead? Are Jews alone in this place? The destination, as with all journeys, is unknown. Yet at the same time, an exile is always shared with others, Jewish and non-Jewish, even if unrecognized by either. Those in exile have particular reasons and circumstances and their history marks them in special ways. Still, the landscape of the exile is also shared and the reasons for exile are as common as they are particular. Who will speak the language that brings this landscape into focus, noting both the particular and shared geography? Will a new language emerge among these exiles who hail from every people and land? Will a destination emerge that can be recognized and embraced as Jewish in solidarity with others who in their exile are also searching out their own identities and possibilities? Or will still another language and identity emerge beyond Judaism and Christianity, beyond any of the known traditions, that one day may recreate the landscape of exile into one of homecoming and justice?

This new landscape is beyond our ability to articulate as our century comes to a close. We know that the future is open even as we often try to define it by our past. That some Jews have entered into exile even as the community celebrates an innocent empowerment testifies to the power of the past, to the extent that the covenantal framework, so violated in the present, continues to nurture the vision of Jews. For why else would these Jews enter the unknown territory, risk unchartered waters, and speak for those whose voices cry out in pain and suffering?

A New Diaspora

In each generation the question of the covenant has to be confronted. Where is the covenant to be found and how it is to be embraced? Is the covenant for the few or the many, for a particular people or for every people? Does the covenant begin with God or with human solidarity? Is God found inside the covenant as its prime mover or does the presence of God emerge from those who gather in solidarity? Are the covenant and God above and beyond history or do both exist within or emerge from the historical moment?

Certainly we know of the different covenantal frameworks that have existed in Biblical and religious history, from Abraham to Noah, from Moses to David, to Jesus and Mohammed. The Abrahamic faiths exist alongside other covenants and religions as well, from Hinduism to Buddhism to native religions around the world. We also now realize how often these covenants have excluded those within its ranks — one thinks here of women in particular — and today a primary religious struggle is to include those who have been excluded and even to chart new religious sensibilities if inclusion in old frameworks cannot be accomplished. There has never been one single covenant nor even two, as is so often spoken of in contemporary Jewish and Christian discourse, but a series of covenants within and beyond these two religions. And, too, these religions, far from representing an essential and unchanging covenant, are themselves an amalgam of differing sensibilities and possibilities. The journeys of Jews and Christians have been as functionally diverse despite the unity claimed by religious leaders. In fact, one might begin an exploration of Judaism and Christianity — as well as other religions — with the question of diversity and shifting definitions of what it means to be Jewish or Christian rather than with the assumption of an initial, never-changing definition worked out over time.

The assumption of a static covenant or, in the modern ecumenical spirit, a series of covenants for particular peoples, assumes a unitary past and a transcendent God who is absent from history. That the Jewish covenant was initially embraced and interpreted by diverse tribes and that the collective that emerged in a journey that featured sojourns, wars, exiles, diasporas, inculturation, and assimilation challenge this notion. The same is true for what we know as Christianity: the diversity of contemporary Christianity, with its many denominations and creeds, is simply an extension of its diverse history since the early followers of Jesus gathered to remember his presence and discern his mission. Like Judaism, Christianity, formed and reformed, has transmuted itself many times in history, including its initial transformation from a gathering of Jews into a world religion.

At the same time, it is clear that Jewish and Christian identity is formed within the context of other identities as well. Because these religious sensibilities have changed over time, and because the primary definition of these religions in the present is always a combination of past and present definitions — with those definitions that have receded always threatening to reappear — Jewish and Christian identity themselves are plural. When coupled with individual, familial, group, geographic, cultural, economic, regional, and national identities, the definition of religion and identity becomes so complex as to be almost unmanageable. With all this diversity found within a previously assumed unity, the burden shifts from a precise and definitive statement of what it means to be Jewish and Christian to how it is possible to speak of religious identity at all.

The changing quality of religious definition and identity is often countered by religious authority and the institutional framework that supports it. In fact the recognition of religious diversity in history and in the present is seen as a threat to be confronted and managed. The threat is found in questioning religious authority and the possibility that if the past is seen in light of circumstance and changing affiliation, then an alternative future may be imagined as well. If the past was open in its own present, if individuals and peoples embraced, divorced, and shifted affiliation and meaning, if the covenant — indeed, covenants — traveled in interpretation and meaning, then the present is unstable as well. History as the defining point when found to be diverse and shifting is subversive to the present and points to a future of unknown destination. For did those tribes who gathered together in their struggle for liberation, who affirmed a God who would be with them in that struggle, do so in order to form a religion called Judaism, with scrolls to read in synagogues, and covenants to be debated over the millennium? Was the religion founded to give aid and comfort to a state that proclaims the fulfillment of its dream in the city of Jerusalem united under Jewish control and virtually emptied of Palestinians? So too with Christianity. Did the followers of the Jewish Jesus, indeed Jesus himself, seek to found a new religion that would for much of its history bless chattel slavery and empire, participate in pogroms, and even provide the foundation for the Holocaust?

If the answers to these questions are obvious, the way forward is less so. Those in exile today from Judaism and Christianity — as well as from other religions — find themselves on common ground carrying their previous religious identity or, because of the perceived violation of these identities, being unable to speak in religious language. The covenant is claimed by the communities they come from and often within the landscape of injustice and oppression. Therefore these exiles are fleeing into uncharted territory often encountering others from their own community and other communities as strangers and without a language to communicate their exile and their hope for the future. In effect, they embody this future in the present with only the suspect language of the past within them and the experience of disappointment and exile linking them.

The stranger aspect is multi-dimensional, for the exile experiences herself as stranger in that she has been forced to leave the familiar space and language of heritage and childhood and then experiences others in the same situation, though they may come from places which are themselves unfamiliar, even historically dangerous to the community from which one hails. If it is difficult enough for Jews to find their critical voice after the Holocaust and within the tremendous pressure of being totally and uncritically committed to Israel, the difficulty increases when a Christian is encountered who is also fleeing his community because of the historic and contemporary injustice of Christian authorities and institutions. A further confrontation is insured when it becomes clear that the imbalance of societal violence and religious legitimation of that violence, obviously weighted in the Christian disfavor, is now being shared by the Jewish community in its legitimation of Israeli policy. That is, where once Christians fled the Christian community because of its propensity toward unjust power and hypocrisy, now Jews are fleeing the Jewish community for the very same reason. A historical shift has occurred in Jewish history that has brought Jews and Christians, once enemies, into a symmetry of complicity and flight.

In this mutual flight the strangers may come to recognize each other in a new way. For thousands of years the recognition has been immediate and unrelenting, as enemy and "other," Jew and Christian have defined themselves over against the other. This has been crucial for the religious authorities of both communities and essential to legitimizing state violence. It has also been important for the silencing of dissenters within both communities, as critical discourse has been defined as traitorous. Looked at another way, the boundaries established by each community have functioned to keep the "other" from discovering the oppressive aspects of each religious system because they are shielded by representing the enemy as being outside. Crossing the boundaries of Judaism and Christianity allows the possibility of seeing the "other" reflected in ones own community and thus recognizing the "other" as more than stranger or, in an obvious way reflecting back to the origins of Judaism and Christianity, as an intimate whose path has crossed one's own in enmity after a difficult birth. However, the point of recognition is not to unfreeze the present by reverting to the past, as if the reality of being "other" in history can be surmounted by recovering a common origin, but by recognizing the injustice of the past and present as throwing exiles together in contemporary life where a future project can be discovered. Returning to the origins is another way of freezing history, as if Jews and Christians are just emerging from the first century of the common era. Instead, the encounter now with all its difficulty and suspicion if taken on its own grounds is a way of moving forward with a common predicament which will spur discussion on many topics, including the past. The openness to a future beyond Judaism and Christianity is a way of subverting the structures that have brought about the exile in the first place. The ecumenical deal has brought Jews and Christians beyond the ecumenical dialogue and such a dialogue in exile is likely to simply replicate old arguments and truces while the future remains to be born. That is why the exile, even after some decades, continues to produce Jews and Christians who, while sharing a similar plight, remain strangers to one another.

Hence Judaism and Christianity haunt these exiles and appear as burdens no one knows how to jettison except in a superficial secularism, an inarticulate rebellion that cannot give birth to a future. In this secularism, where the covenant is ignored or derided, is the question of fidelity. Those who remain identified as Jews and Christians belittle the secularists and debate the religious in a way that rarely promotes life or answers the most perplexing questions of the exilic community. Are those in exile to be in an eternal middle, battling those who do not speak of faith and those who do? Does identification with those who speak of faith and sanction injustice require distance from those who refuse religious language and yet work for justice? Of course, the distance from faith hardly guarantees a decided option for those outside the systems of power. Thus, the exile is not decided along the old lines of Jew and Christian or even religious and secular. Rather the exilic community is composed of those who are fleeing from contemporary injustice and hope to build a world beyond what is known today. Secular and religious, Jew and Christian, are no longer the defining labels.

When exiles begin to recognize one another — which in another way is recognizing oneself — then a condition of flight gives way to the possibility of solidarity. The present situation opens a possible future and the movement of exile into a diaspora community. Diaspora is dispersion within the context of community; it is a movement away from empire and oppression toward the creation of a new matrix of values and institutions. The past is brought with those who form the new diaspora but only as possibilities, remnants, small contributions to be combined, confronted, transmuted with other pasts. The present defines the community more strongly than the past, as mutuality of experience is the guide for sifting through values and actions. Interaction in the present brings a recognition of parts of the past that must be jettisoned and those parts that have been abused and perverted which might be preserved or reconfigured.

One thinks here of the question of salvation in Christianity or the sense of Jewish redemption in Israel. Though differing in duration and context, both the claims of salvation and redemption are disasters for those on the other side of the claims. If both are held as the highest value *and* are disasters then the very concepts themselves need to be revaluated. Furthermore, the recognition that disaster for the "other" is likewise disaster for those who make the claim — for is not this the reason for the exile itself? — is a humbling moment that connects the "other" and those from the community who make the claim in a new way. The re-evaluation is itself a way of confession and reconciliation especially when it is done in the face of, and with, the "other." In a long history peoples oppress and are oppressed, claims to redemption are made and experienced, exiles are begun and aborted. Thus in every history all of these elements of complicity and oppression are experienced and when the confession and reconciliation are authentic then the humility of the most recently oppressed can surface as well. Even the attempt to freeze the relationship of victim and oppressor, thus denying the capacity of both to change or be culpable, gives way before a genuine grappling with the issues and capacities of life shared by all.

Here we can approach in a genuine way the possibility of forgiveness. Forgiveness as a mutual accounting of the past and the present frees the person and the community to the possibility of a new future. When authentic, forgiveness is preceded by a confession that is searching and reflective rather than simply damning and univocal. Like the present, the past is complex in its various configurations and the potentialities of violence and deceit are the same that confront the future that is hoped for. The tendency toward fidelity and betrayal are common patterns, even if adorned with specific symbols for particular epochs and peoples, and the very dichotomy itself may be part of the inability to move forward. Authentic forgiveness is mutual in that the cycle of fidelity and betrayal is identified and then seen in a larger context of a journey that is diverse in its content and intent. In this journey the good and bad can be identified, but unless a more complex and ambivalent picture emerges, unless the dichotomy of victor and victim gives way, then the past is woven into the present as the defining point of the future. But at that point too often the victor and victim have changed places, for is it possible to condemn forever and maintain a reflective view on life that is self-critical? Can a future be created without the ability to forgive and be forgiven, and even to move beyond the need for forgiveness to see a depth of life from which we emerge and to which we seek to journey forward?

The Christian theologian Carter Heyward and the Jewish philosopher Hannah Arendt have emphasized the need for forgiveness as a way of embarking on a path toward justice and reconciliation. Heyward terms this "revolutionary forgiveness," a process of forgiveness in which the righting of the wrong that has been done is given priority. The righting of wrong is itself a process of self-discovery and change and becomes with the act of forgiveness a way of viewing the world as it is transformed in confession and justice. In this journey a healing begins to take place within and between those who were once strangers and enemies. The creation of a different future is essential to enable forgiveness to realize its authenticity and reach its revolutionary potential, for without the movement toward justice, forgiveness is simply a piety without substance that leaves the world as it is. The freeing of the future, of course, means a forgiveness that acts critically with the past and seeks to minimize that which originally gave rise to the offense in the first place.

Arendt's caution about forgiveness is important here. For Arendt, there are some crimes in the public realm which are so heinous that they exist outside the framework of the human and therefore cannot be forgiven. One thinks of the Holocaust in this regard and here the challenge is simply to forge a new path beyond the terrible nature of that atrocity. The tragedy of the Holocaust is exacerbated by the generation after, not because it refuses to forgive but because in the holding up of that tragedy self-critical reflection is diminished. The community chooses a path which to some extent replicates the paths of others that have violated the community in the past. Instead of embarking on a new venture, the Jewish community seeks survival and security in the most obvious of ways: territorial and national sovereignty. The consequence for the Palestinian people is obvious and the cycle of pain and suffering continues. One may argue that the pain of the Holocaust is extended to the Palestinians and at the same time that the healing that Jews pursued through empowerment has been illusory. Could it be that the cycle of dislocation and death continued by Jews after the Holocaust has increased the trauma of the Jewish people itself? Creating a future that in important ways replicates the past is more than a refusal of forgiveness for an unforgivable event. Rather it extends the unforgivable act to another people not responsible for the original injury. The trap is obvious and one that Arendt knew only too well: life cannot be defined by the unforgivable or lived indefinitely within its shadow. The task is to move on with those who will journey with you, but first the desire to move internally must be manifest. Carrying the Holocaust as a sign of distinction is a recipe for isolation and mistrust. Trust cannot be earned within the context of an event beyond even the ability to punish, nor can healing be achieved.

Forgiveness is thus provisional, less a definitive act than a posture of critical reflection and openness to a future beyond the past. Arendt stresses that the act of forgiveness itself is a realization of the complexity and limitations of life, as well as a release from grief. The act has future consequences for identity, culture, and politics that cannot be known in the present. Insofar as forgiveness is possible within the movement of a new solidarity, the shared history of the adversaries remains so, but in a new configuration. In the West, the example of Jews and Christians after the Holocaust exemplifies this process. Once bitter adversaries, a new relationship of trust and mutuality has grown up. The transformed relationship is multi-faceted and may involve a solidarity against new "enemies." Clearly part of the Jewish-Christian relationship in the present is an agreement to share the spoils of Western capitalism; in some quarters Jews can be elevated into full participation in the white and Western, domination over other races and cultures. Forgiveness here is a deal to resolve one injustice and unite to perpetrate further injustices with a clear conscience. The "other" disappears to create a different "other" more convenient and more important in the present. Still, the new relationship may develop a critical matrix from which Jews and Christians can recognize a constantly evolving estrangement and that the task is to be vigilant in recognizing that resolution of one enmity may lead to still another projection of otherness. A solidarity devoutly wished for may lead to solidarity against a new enemy.

This can only occur if the past and present are frozen, as if the warring parties, now friends, inhabit the center of history. If Christianity sees itself as the center of history and therefore seeks to displace Jews, a history of suffering is created. If at the end of this travail, Christians recognize the cost of this understanding and therefore elevate Jews to this center as well — a center that Jews themselves have claimed — then the triumphal sensibility, undermined by suffering, is now resurrected. In this sense, confession and forgiveness are used to reestablish a legitimacy once threatened by critical consciousness. The challenge of the diaspora is different. It refuses to re-establish a link with a power that seeks to substitute one people's suffering for another's. But it can only do this by decentering Jewish and Christian history and by refusing the alluring prospect of security in joining the victor. Stripped of pious and memorial rhetoric, perhaps this is what Jewish leadership is saying to Jewish dissenters: that the ecumenical deal allows Jews to finally join the circle of power that only recently threatened them with annihilation. The ecumenical deal is therefore not about Israel at all but a fundamental survival strategy in a culture defined by Christianity. If Christianity is to be militant, if the cycle of quiescence is typically followed by renewed aggression, let it be against someone else. Let Jews benefit from the resolution of the civil war between Jews and Christians and use the strength and affluence of the Christian West to benefit the Jewish community, particularly in Israel. Jewish dissenters threaten the ultimate deal, the survival deal, that allows Jews to join the Christian West while claiming a history of innocence and suffering. It is the best of all worlds, benefitting from exploitation with the pretense of innocence. Could the penalty for dissenting with Israeli policies be so harsh because it is really a penalty for breaking with the unspoken code of survival with Christians in the West?

After this history of suffering, who could argue with such a deal? Though certainly understandable, the deal is hypocritical for Jews and Christians because neither discuss the underlying intent of this solidarity. For Jews it is a method of survival; for Christians a way of providing legitimation for their conscience and assuring continued dominance. Still the exiles from both communities testify to those who choose another way and who are willing to continue to confront the new "others" of Jewish and Christian life. By refusing to live within the post-Holocaust deal between the Jewish and Christian communities, and by their willingness to confront and listen to each other, these exiles are critically evaluating the present. In fact, the diaspora community is a continual confrontation and listening as new "others" present themselves — Palestinians and Latin Americans for example — in an ever-expanding network of relations. Palestinians confront Jews in the most obvious way, suggesting that Jews live after the Holocaust *and* the state of Israel, but they also confront Christians in the West, suggesting that their silence and complicity in regard to the Holocaust is now complemented by their silence and complicity in regard to the Palestinian catastrophe. Latin Americans who suffer massive poverty and underemployment inform Jewish and Christian understandings that they both benefit from an economic and political system that distorts the distribution of wealth and power. Peace between Jews and Christians in North America, for example, is found at great cost to others who now exist on the other side of this peace. The diaspora community is confronted with an ever-evolving series of relationships that question even the obvious benefits of a monumentally important truce.

Letting Go of the Covenant

If the covenant and its obligations need to be thought through in every generation, then the new diaspora must confront this problem as well. At least in Jewish history, the dispersion of the people has led to radical revisions of the covenant. This is true because the history which confronted the people raised questions which the old interpretation of the covenant could not answer. Of course, responses to history have always been diverse, and within the context of cultures apart from the exilic culture. Yet despite this long history of exile and reinterpretation, the situation is different today. It is almost as if a certain phase of Jewish and Christian history has come to a close, as if the trajectory of foundational histories has run its course. The new critical ecumenism is an interaction of diverse traditions and cultures that cannot revive or renew in a cyclical manner as the length of these histories, their participation in atrocity, the critical recovery of the origins of the communities, the discovery of the "other" as intimate and proximate, all force the covenant to a new level. The point is no longer the embrace of "the" covenant but rather the question of what can be affirmed in the creation of a future worth bequeathing to coming generations. The point does not so much hark back to the origins of the different covenants as it discerns what is left of the covenants to be affirmed.

The search for the origins of the covenants within the traces left in the present is quite different from the typical search for the renewal of the covenant within particular communities. Confronted with others and in solidarity with them, covenants become places of discussion and debate, points of departure and ending, analysis of original and historical dynamics. Particular covenants give way before the larger array of possible affirmations and the way of affirmation, because of the diversity, tends to be small rather than grandiose. To some, this may seem to diminish the grandeur of the covenants and render great moments in history insignificant. Yet on reflection, was this not the birthing place of the covenants we now deem significant? To the Egyptian and Canaanite societies, the Jewish covenant must have seemed insignificant, weak, beside the point, ridiculous, as did the Christian covenant to Jewish and Roman society. The origins of the Enlightenment covenant was similarly weak in the face of medieval religious and secular authorities. That they arose within a certain historical moment, were precarious in their birth and uncertain in their future is often lost today when speaking of the movements and authority patterns that loom large in our time even as they lose their power to orient peoples. The very search for the origins of the covenants remind those in the diaspora today that the birth of covenants is possible, as is their death. The birth of Judaism and Christianity happened within established orders and at the same time signaled a death for other forms that tried to claim the future as theirs.

Recovering the origins of the covenants within the context of the new diaspora is a sharing of insights and potentialities. In some ways we have reached the end of Judaism and Christianity — and the Enlightenment as well — though we are surrounded by their symbolism and patterns of thought. Instead of leaving behind what continues to exist, the challenge is to carry forward what remains even as it is reconfigured. What is carried forward is disciplined and humbled, an interior reality rather than one proclaimed as definitive. In the face of the "other" who has experienced the proclamation as a form of oppression, and now in a solidarity with the "other" who has ceased to be defined as such, and with the intimate knowledge that the suffering at the hands of your community's proclamation has also led to the end of that proclamation within your own sensibility, the experience of the Jewish and Christian covenants can only be found within. Though this seems to minimize its impact and importance, the interior path can clarify the public contribution of covenants that can no longer be announced publicly. Further, the covenant that clarifies a person's vision and has no claim on others can be freely shared because the necessity of unifying others around this covenant has receded. Non-attachment to the spread and proclamation of the covenant one holds allows it to freely mingle with other perspectives, informing and learning in a dynamic serving a larger cause. If covenants have been primarily seen as ways of symbolizing and ordering the human journey, this function remains in a changed atmosphere. The ordering is now done within the interaction of the covenants out of which may grow a new covenant. No longer is the concern of a covenantal framework simply to reproduce itself, and the exilic community relinquishes the responsibility of carrying on a tradition that has come to an end.

Why at the point of a chosen path would exiles seek to reproduce their covenant in their own image? Does one come into exile simply to testify to the authenticity of one's own vision? Or in exile does the vision of authenticity change? The diaspora reality cautions that the notion of the "authentic" covenant is part of the problem from which exiles have fled. The quest for authenticity reduces the diaspora community and the meeting of the "other" to a strategic necessity, to once again divide among those who carry one covenant or another. The cycle is therefore ready to repeat itself, as the notion of exclusive covenant is affirmed even by those in exile. In this sense the exiled are simply there waiting to return to their community of origin or bring their community to the "proper" understandings. Exile is a functional reality, bound by circumstance with the sole aim to accomplish certain goals. Can this be seen as an honest reckoning with the history that brought about the exile in the first place? If the new diaspora is simply a place to straighten things out, to reconfigure the covenant into a more likable framework, then the suffering caused by the communities of origin is minimized, becoming a platform for confession and continuance. Just as the ecumenical dialogue became a deal, so too does the exile become a deal where confession and transformation are strategic and the promotion of certain interests reigns supreme. In reality, just as the ecumenical deal becomes a partnership in changing and reviving the leadership of the communities, so does the exilic deal becomes a tool to promote new establishments in the Jewish and Christian communities.

Perhaps the diaspora community must search for a provisional covenant, one characterized by transition and openness. Or it might be called a diaspora covenant since the framework that comes into being will have a specific historical focus. Upon reflection, however, it is startling how this formation of one covenant is similar to others previously formed, for the latter likewise came into being in exile, emerging among disparate groups and peoples searching for a way forward. And just as these ancient covenants built upon and diverged from previous covenants, so, too, does the covenant that is forming today. The risk taken by early Jews and Christians is similar to the one taken today: a risk for the future because the past is no longer adequate for the present. The risk for the future rests on the danger posed by continuance of the old. The danger is multi-faceted and includes the realization that by carrying that which is no longer adequate into the future, the very relationship with God and each other is jeopardized.

For was the purpose of the covenant to embrace *forever* a particular self-understanding, with laws, rituals, and beliefs, or was it to facilitate a deep entry into the history of a particular time with a particular people to accomplish a particular project? The reification of that calling into particular religions served a purpose, for the contact of the moment, monumental and beyond the generation that experienced it, could be preserved. But was that moment to be preserved simply to be recited and reproduced until the end of time, and even as the preservation wandered from the initial impulse to the crusades, to colonialism, to the Holocaust, to the displacement of Palestinians, and beyond to the killing fields of Cambodia, Bosnia, and Rwanda? Tradition as preservation of the formative event that gave rise to these movements of transformation — and after all, is this not what the formation of Judaism, Christianity, Islam, Buddhism, the Enlightenment, were in their origins? — is important because it rescues the essence of certain moments of transcendence and transformation as testimony to the possibility of other moments arising. Tradition preserves, to be sure, but to reproduce the tradition simply as a rote exercise or out of fear of the future is to take the explosive moment it preserves and domesticate it. The diaspora is the spawning ground for a new covenant because of the many traditions the diaspora encompasses and places together in this moment of historical crisis. Mix multitudes and covenants in the diaspora of our time and the result is bound to be explosive. Still the point is not innovation or radical change in itself. Rather it is coming together in a time in history when the next step in all areas of life, including in religiosity, must be taken.

God is Now

The question of God haunts this discussion, underlies it, and, paradoxically — some may think, inappropriately — is the last to be addressed. Like the covenant, however, God is found in the mix of history,
emerges from history, and is often articulated within or just after the
moment of crisis. The canonical writings in Judaism and Christianity
bear this out, as do all canonical writings of world and indigenous religions. The proclamations and creeds are always *after* the revelation, or
one might say, after the historical moment that has called a community into being. Canonical writings as well as those writings excluded
from the canon are reflections on the event and the role of God to be
discerned there. Tradition is a further reflection on or refinement of
the story to be remembered and emulated. As we know, the canon and
the tradition are also ways of owning and sometimes perverting the
historical message. At the same time, the explosive message of God as
perceived by the early followers is preserved, embellished upon, ritual-
ized, and sometimes lost. Often as not, for the message to be found,
tradition must be sifted through carefully and with an intensity that
belies the original intention of the formation of the community. God is
now, often at the core of the covenants, a God who is difficult to access,
a sermonic God carried through layers of ritual and archaic language,
the same God whom the founders of these religions sought to escape.
The God who encouraged movement and risk and promised to be found
in the creation of a future different from the past becomes a God who
does the opposite, counseling quiescence and security. The God of the
past is most often the God encountered in Judaism and Christianity.

For those who came together to form the Jewish and Christian communities, the God of the past was abandoned, sometimes reluctantly,
for a God whom they encountered but had difficulty identifying. Who
was this God who spoke of liberation of slaves, who promised to be with
them in their flight and struggle? The Hebrew Bible recounts stories of
what the people thought this God to be, only to be face disappointment
or surprise. The Christian scriptures can be seen in this light as well:
the Jewish God who now was known, or at least thought to be known,
took on aspects that surprised and divided Jews and later Christians
themselves. God as an evolving concept and reality is clearly seen in
the Testaments even as many claimed to know the final understanding, or that the truth they had come to understand had never changed.
Identification and definition of God are thus constantly elusive, changing, surprising, and subverting those who claim knowledge of the divine. Tradition is therefore holding back, reigning in, organizing God
so as to be owned and handed down. Is it therefore surprising that the
God proclaimed by Jews and Christians is often the God of the past?

The God found in the new diaspora is a God of the future. Coming

from the past and breaking with it — at the same time carrying elements of the past in the present — the challenge is to continue on
without certainty and security. The failure of Jewish and Christian
dissent is important to consider and then to move beyond, as appeals
to the wider Jewish and Christian community are necessary and, at
the same time, secondary in importance. Alliances with those of the
original community are crucial yet frayed; looking back to the communities left behind can only be strategic and tenuous. This, too, with the
God of the past on whom the Jewish and Christian establishments continue to call. The words of fidelity to this God can be spoken for strategic reasons, but that speech is empty, almost a betrayal of the insights
and the community forming in the diaspora. Can Jews identify with
the Jewish community, come into solidarity with Jewish causes, speak
the words of love and affection for Israel, raise the specter of anti-
Semitism as a watchword for the Jewish world in order to gain the
"credentials" to speak in the name of Jewish history, while remaining
faithful to the exilic journey they have already embarked upon? Can
Christians speak in the language of the Christian tradition, proclaim
the uniqueness of the Christian gospel, mouth the words of the patri-
archal God and be faithful to their journey beyond exclusiveness and
atrocity? The speech of the past invokes the God of the past and thus
the formation of the new diaspora and the God who will emerge from
there is delayed. Those in the diaspora reach back in strategy *and* in
fear of the path they have embarked upon. This, too, is Biblical in its
sensibilities, with the exodus from Egypt being accompanied by the
desire for the security of slavery.

Perhaps the bridge between the previous reality and the one that is
coming into being is found in an unfamiliar tension of the ancient covenants with the covenant that will be. The ancient covenants, even in
their symbolic presentation by the hierarchy of Judaism and Christianity, hold a memory of God's presence and activity in history. This
memory is haunting in its dimensions and power. For many this memory
— and its abuse in the present — is the reason for embarking on the
exile itself, for how is it that those who leave the comfortable worlds of
Judaism and Christianity continue to search for a religious dimension
to their lives? Why choose exile if not for a reason beyond comfort and
security? Yet a retreat into memory is a betrayal of the subversive aspect of the memory itself. The covenants and God of the past propels
many toward a covenant and a God of the future, thus representing a
one-way bridge. If God is now, then the ancient God is within the now,
though transformed in the history and the diaspora community of our
time. To return in language and concept to the covenants and God of
the past for strategic or security concerns is to return to a place that no
longer exists. It is like returning to a museum of memories, visiting an
ancient cathedral or synagogue, posturing through nostalgia.

Diaspora Dissent

The battle of dissent with state power appears a perpetually losing proposition, especially in the face of the power of the modern state. The loss is worldwide and escalating, and the power of religion seems bent on legitimating that power until it finds a new one worthy of support. The strategic positioning of religious institutions and authority is both historic and shameless. It is here where the betrayal of the covenants is most obvious and devastating. More than any other reason, this betrayal gives birth to exiles from every corner of the globe. Should it surprise us that Palestinian empowerment, as limited and circumscribed as it is under the Oslo accords, has produced its own exiles? Disappointment with the Palestinian authority, especially with Yasir Arafat and the returning members of the PLO, is growing and the charges of corruption, collaboration, exploitation, authoritarianism, and torture are now made almost routinely. Since 1993 another Palestinian diaspora has come into being, within Palestine and in the Palestinian diaspora created in 1948.

The diaspora is two-fold, one created by Israel, the other self-generated. The former exists within a geographical space, mostly the Middle East; the other takes its place among other exiles, including Jews, in the new diaspora. Edward Said's harsh criticism of the Palestinian Authority is distrusted and censored by the Authority even as it resonates among others who have been exiled in their own time. Said's critique can be interpreted in many ways, though the overall tone and sensibility is clear: a profound disappointment, even to the point of betrayal, of the hope that his people would lay the groundwork for a different moral and political order in the Middle East and beyond. Comparisons with the hope and disappointment of Jews are easy and to a large extent true, for Jews and Palestinians hoped that suffering and forced exile would help bring about a new order in the world that would never again provide the groundwork for what their people had suffered. To say that disappointment with empowerment is inevitable does not soften the blow to those who struggle on behalf of ideals and their own people. Nor does it mean a quietism, as if defeat is inevitable and the struggle for victory to be shunned. Rather, the struggle is joined from a different perspective, with different values, responsibilities, and loyalties. The failure of dissent in Jewish and Palestinian life, for example, has resulted from a sense that the question of justice and identity can somehow be resolved within the framework of the nation-state. Of course, many within both communities have seen the nation-state as a place of rescue from forced exile and diaspora, and with the histories of both peoples, who could judge this a mistake? What else in the modern world could promise relief from suffering at the hands of others, themselves organized within nation-states? Those who have been conquered and colonized, those who have been thrown off their land and herded into refugee and concentration camps and worse, have little choice but to see their future in the very system that has done so much damage to them. The desire for the "normalization" of Jewish and Palestinian life runs through both histories and for good reason, but the other side of normalization is the experience of injustice within the "solution" to the problem of displacement and destruction. Joining the family of nations on an equal and respectable footing is to participate in the very same things that negatively impacted one's own people. Foreign alliances are joined and expanded often at the expense of others who are suffering, just as domestic policies often benefit the elite and relegate others to poverty.

Normalization is a two-edge sword whose consequences are difficult to predict and, even more importantly, almost impossible to restrain once the state apparatus is in place. Arguments about the evil of the occupier and the murderers quickly shift to the *realpolitik* of dissenting within the mainstream society. Examples from Israel are easy enough to produce and they keep multiplying. The ghettoization of Jews is protested endlessly even as the ghettoization of Palestinians proceeds. Innocent Jewish suffering is memorialized even as the Israeli bombing of innocent Lebanese in Beirut escalates. Nazis humiliating Jews is borne with great sorrow and anger at the very time that Jewish soldiers humiliate Palestinians in their homes and villages. This is hardly confined to Israel. Today, Palestinians wonder about the usurpation of their aspirations and values by the Palestinian Authority and compare this experience to the Israeli occupation. Corruption and torture, the turning of a national struggle into a political and economic game for the elite, is found to be as prevalent among Palestinians as they once thought it as defining about Jews.

Yet the scope of this disaffection is much wider than Israel and Palestine. The exile includes many who have been separated from nation-states and others who are in exile within those entities. Some continue to address the problems of injustice through language and symbolism that no longer applies to the situation. They hope to reform the structures through a return to the original impetus of the traditions that legitimize the state. They, too, accept normalization and argue within it but, as with the situation in Israel and Palestine, the stakes continue to escalate. Less is held out as possible and less is demanded. It is almost as if nation-states and dissenters are in a downward spiral, continuing to argue in the same paradigms as the world continues on.

The failure of dissent thus goes well beyond the small but significant geography of Israel and Palestine. In the era of Netanyahu, but before and after as well, the prospects for a significant change in outlook are dim. Still, the challenge remains there as elsewhere, and it may be that one can only witness to the hope of justice and reconciliation in our time. Revolutionary forgiveness may be possible to model only in small ways in a diaspora still forming and as yet without a clear direction. Perhaps the diaspora will lack direction until the world situation becomes even worse and the consciousness of the increasing population in the diaspora is raised beyond present day levels. Unfortunately, it seems the case that only a disaster is what motivates many into searching out alternatives in a serious way, and these alternatives are only truly alternative to the systems in place when the system itself has failed completely. Of course there is no guarantee that the succeeding system will offer a way out of the situation. Often as not, old divisions and injustices are remedied by creating new divisions and injustices. The revolutionary potential of collapse, forgiveness, reconciliation, and justice is held up as an ideal as it is lost in actual practice. Those in exile often see the new order as the way to end their exile, to reintegrate into a homeland that promises home and security. Their reintegration is often purchased at the price of a new exile and the formation of a new diaspora.

Does the God of the diaspora travel with those who return home? Does the covenant they carry simply replace the one they fled, replicating for others the pain originally experienced? Can diaspora dissent return home and continue in its critique until the society has changed in its inner core and institutional configuration? Or do the God, covenant, and dissent of the diaspora live in the diaspora, awaiting the arrival of the new exiles to begin again the search for a world beyond injustice?

Perhaps the diaspora is like God, perpetually arguing for a future that does not arrive. Or perhaps the diaspora, like God, is a witness to a future which could be *and* is already when those who choose exile and those who are in exile without choice face one another in pain and hope. In this sense God and the future are now, before us, here.

10

Toward an Arab-Jewish Humanism

by Muhammad Hallaj

One of the principal reasons why the Palestinian-Israeli peace process has been controversial among Palestinians, and why Palestinian public opinion has been ambivalent toward the Oslo accords and subsequent agreements reached by the PLO with the government of Israel, is that they left the Palestinian future as uncertain and the Palestinian national movement as vulnerable as ever. Mahmoud Abbas (Abu Mazen), the PLO leader who played a major role in negotiating the PLO agreements with Israel, and who signed the first Oslo agreement on behalf of the Palestinians in Washington on September 13, 1993, himself recognized the uncertainty of the Palestinian future under the Oslo agreement. The agreement, he told the press shortly after the signing of the Oslo accord amidst much fanfare on the lawn of the White House, represents another crossroads for the Palestinian people, because it carries in its belly the promise of Palestinian independence as well as the threat of continued Israeli occupation.

The first Oslo agreement, which laid the ground rules for future Palestinian-Israeli negotiations, concerned itself only with "interim arrangements" and deferred the principal substantive issues — called "final status issues" (including the future of Jerusalem and Jewish settlements, the rights of Palestinian refugees, borders between Israel and the Palestinian territories) — to future negotiations. While the process was very specific about the desired outcome for Israel (Arab recognition, peace agreements, and normalization of relations), it left the desired outcome for the Palestinians unspecified and at the mercy of unpredictable future negotiations.

In a way, Arab-Israeli negotiations, designed by former U.S. Secretary of State James Baker and inaugurated amidst much optimism in Madrid at the end of October 1991, were unlike anything in the annals of international diplomacy. Antagonists who decide to embark on conflict resolution normally agree on the desired outcome of diplomacy (e.g., to end nuclear weapons testing in the atmosphere), then negotiate how and under what conditions to attain the desired and agreed objective. The diplomatic exercise designed by Mr. Baker specified the desired outcome for one of the parties and left the outcome for the other parties to be whatever the process produced in the end.

The Palestinians wanted Israel to recognize their nationhood, to agree to terminate its 25-year occupation and to allow the emergence of an independent Palestinian state in the West Bank and Gaza Strip, alongside Israel. They agreed to enter the negotiations under the assumption that the agreed framework for the negotiations (UN Security Council Resolution 242, based on the principle of the "inadmissibility of the acquisition of territory by war" and the principle of "exchange of land for peace") favored the outcome that they desired. They were also encouraged by the fact that the large majority of the world's nations favored the sort of outcome that the Palestinians themselves desired, as evidenced by many United Nations resolutions endorsing the establishment of a Palestinian state in the West Bank and Gaza Strip. The fact that Israel demanded Palestinian recognition of Israeli nationhood and independence in advance without granting the Palestinians equal recognition bothered the Palestinians but did not keep them from entering the negotiations anyway.

The uncertainty of the Palestinian future, rooted in an open-ended political process, is compounded by the fact that, during its 30 years of occupation of the Palestinian territories of the West Bank (including Arab Jerusalem) and Gaza Strip, Israel's policies (particularly its policy of building Jewish colonies on confiscated Palestinian land) created a geopolitical scenario designed to make it difficult or even impossible to extricate the Palestinians from Israeli control. The purpose, of course, was to make Israeli withdrawal from the West Bank and Gaza difficult and painful and to make the emergence of an independent Palestinian state in these territories impractical. Such policies were the practical dimension of Israel's policy of denying Palestinian nationhood.

The asymmetry of power between the two parties in the political process being negotiated reinforced the already existing tilt in favor of Israel, making it practically impossible for the Palestinians to secure anything resembling the national future that they desired. Subjective and objective conditions surrounding the negotiations over the Palestinian future conspired to make it unpredictable whether it is national freedom that awaits at the end of the road or the legitimization of perpetual occupation and exile.

Subsequent agreements between the Palestinians and Israel seemed to confirm the fears of the critics of the peace process that the Palestinian future being fashioned by the Palestinian-Israeli agreements under the Oslo formula would fall far short of the desired outcome of self-determination and independent statehood. The Taba agreement (Oslo II) signed by the PLO and Israel in September 1995 fragmented the Palestinian territories into three zones: Zone A comprising the main Palestinian cities (and only six percent of the land), from which Israeli troops were to be withdrawn and which were to be turned over to a "Palestinian authority"; Zone B, which was to be jointly administered by Israel and the Palestinian authority pending future phased redeployment of Israeli troops; Zone C (including most of the territory of the West Bank) which is to remain under Israeli control until future negotiations produce an agreement on their fate. Israeli leaders quickly made no secret of the fact that Zone C (including 60 percent of the West Bank) was the territory that Israel intended to annex and to claim sovereignty over when "final status" negotiations began.

What this means is that the future Israel envisions for the Palestinian people is something very much like the status accorded Africans during the days of apartheid in South Africa. In fact, it became fashionable to refer to the territories under the Palestinian "self rule" regime as "bantustans." The fragmentation of the West Bank, producing Palestinian "autonomous" territories surrounded by larger areas reserved for Israeli Jewish colonists and under the jurisdiction of the Israeli state, precludes a coherent national life for the Palestinians, both geographically and demographically. Statehood under such conditions would be unattainable, and a viable socio-economic national life for the Palestinians would be impractical. Palestinians would in effect live within "reservations" with limited autonomy and ringed by an Israeli-Jewish presence. And it would all happen under the illusion of Arab-Jewish reconciliation blessed by international acquiescence.

It is not difficult to extrapolate the sort of future that awaits the Palestinian people at the end of the present peace process if it were to mature into final agreement along the lines of accords reached so far. The Palestinians would be in nominal control ("limited self-rule") in a fraction of the territories they inhabited when Israel seized them from Jordan in the Arab-Israeli war of 1967. Furthermore, such territories would be fragmented into isolated enclaves and surrounded by Jewish settlements under Israeli jurisdiction and possibly sovereignty. Half of the Palestinian people, made refugees during the original Arab-Israeli war of 1948 and displaced persons from the war of 1967, would be rendered permanent exiles to be eventually resettled in the surrounding Arab countries where they initially took refuge.

Needless to say, the sort of Palestinian future which is likely to emerge from the present political process is more likely to perpetuate the Arab-Israeli conflict than to end it. It leaves the Palestinian grievance intact because it would leave the Palestinian people a non-self-governing people, and essentially a nation in exile. These were the original grievances which ignited the conflict and kept it going during the past five decades, and they are not likely to serve now as the basis for reconciliation. Even if an overwhelming imbalance of power and the force of compelling regional and international circumstances were to make the Palestinians enter into such agreements, they will be viewed by future Palestinian and Arab generations as diktats signed under duress without moral or legal force, a condition bound to lead to the resumption of the conflict as soon as circumstances permit.

A more optimistic view of the current peace process, however, envisions a more generous outcome: the two-state solution that would herald Arab-Jewish coexistence and conciliation. For Israel, it envisions the end of Arab belligerency, the acceptance of the Jewish state of Israel as a legitimate Middle Eastern state, and the establishment of normal relations between it and other countries in the region, conditions which would grant Israel the security that victories in war have failed to secure for it, and the prosperity which is unattainable without peaceful and normal relations between Israel and the Arab world. For the Arabs, the peace process would restore lands occupied by Israel since the war of 1967, would remove a major irritant in the Arabs' relations with the western powers, and for the Palestinians it would mean the end of foreign occupation and the advent of the self-determination of which they have been deprived and for which they have struggled for half a century.

It is not surprising that an international consensus evolved around the two-state solution. It was in line with the original 1947 United Nations resolution to partition Palestine into Arab and Jewish states, and in line with numerous General Assembly resolutions on the Palestine question, calling for Palestinian self-determination, adopted during the past 20 years, giving it "international legitimacy," just as the partition resolution gave such "legitimacy" to Israel. It also seemed to coincide, more than other possible solutions, with the prevailing notion of fairness to the parties. The two state solution also seemed to enjoy greater acceptance by substantial constituencies within Arab and Israeli societies than alternative outcomes. In fact it is the only solution to the Arab-Israeli conflict which both sides have endorsed, albeit at different times: by the Jews in 1947, when it was first proposed, and since 1974 by the Arabs. Furthermore, it requires the least drastic adjustment to the status quo and the least painful change in the present realities of the region. And as a bonus, it is generally perceived as the key to peace in the Middle East. It is understandable, then, that the two-state solution would appear to be the most practical and fair solution to the Arab-Israeli conflict, and the most desirable outcome to the present peace process.

For these reasons, the Palestinian future is most commonly seen in terms of a mini- Palestinian state in the West Bank and Gaza Strip (about 20 percent of historic Palestine), coexisting with the Jewish state of Israel in the rest of the disputed land. This is the optimistic vision of the outcome of the present peace process, not yet assured since Israel has yet to accept such a result, although it is clear that a substantial segment of Israeli public opinion is willing to live with it. But it is the minimum below which no stable peace is possible, because a less generous outcome would leave too much of the Palestinian grievance unredressed, and therefore politically unacceptable to the Arab side.

It is the contention of this essay, however, that even though it may be argued that the two-state solution is the best possible outcome to the ongoing Arab-Israeli peace process, it is not the most desirable future for the Palestinians or the Israelis or the Middle East. It is also the contention of this essay that the two-state solution ought to be seen as the beginning and not the end of the Arab-Jewish reconciliation process, because its greatest virtue is that it opens greater future possibilities for Arab-Jewish coexistence in the Holy Land and a more stable peace in the Middle East.

What is wrong with the two-state solution? It is not sufficiently daring as a vision for the future of the Palestinian and Israeli peoples. It represents the dream of small minds held captive by current political convenience at the expense of greater future possibility. It is a desirable outcome of current negotiations because it diminishes grievances to make it possible to terminate or at least to suspend the Arab-Israeli conflict, but it falls short of what is needed to consummate the metamorphosis of Arab-Jewish relations into a historic reconciliation.

Its principal shortcomings include the fact that both the Palestinian Arabs and Israeli Jews would be excluded from a part of what they consider to be their historic homeland. The Palestinians would be aliens in nearly 80 percent of what has been until recently historic Palestine, and the Israeli Jews would be aliens in what they call "Judea and Samaria," parts of what is to them the "land of Israel." In addition, half of the Palestinian people, the present refugees, are not likely to be repatriated to Israel, their original home, and it would be impractical to absorb them in the mini-Palestine in the already densely populated and territorially limited West Bank and Gaza. They will continue to be a volatile element threatening the stability of the host Arab countries where they would be required to remain; they will detract from the legitimacy of the Palestinian state which abandons them and betrays their rights, and they will continue to threaten the stability of Arab-Israeli peace with irredentist aspirations and revolutionary struggles. Palestine and Israel, both small and poor in natural resources, will become increasingly non-viable in a world of expanding political and economic units.

Before long, both Israel and Palestine would become increasingly unsatisfying to their respective citizens (economically, emotionally, and eventually politically), and the efficacy and the legitimacy of the partition of Palestine into Arab and Jewish mini-states will again be brought into question. The two-state solution will have served a transitional historic purpose, but it will exhaust its value and it will need to be superseded by something less ephemeral and transitory in its capacity to fulfill the aspirations of the peoples of the Holy Land.

Fortunately, such a scenario exists, although the raging national-ism of our time, much like tribalism in its exclusivism, makes it tempo-rarily beyond the political and emotional capacities of the parties. It involves the reconstruction of the Holy Land as a binational republic in which Palestinian Arabs (both Muslims and Christians) and Israeli Jews share a common homeland with equal rights and obligations.

The binational Arab-Jewish republic is not a novel idea, and it may not be an idea whose time has come, but it is an idea whose time will come, and it serves the best interests of both sides to prepare for it. Advocates of binationalism — as the more humane and civilized way out of the Arab-Jewish struggle over Palestine — have come from both sides. Initially, in the 1940s when the Arab-Jewish struggle was ap-proaching a crisis, binationalism was advocated by a minority of Jew-ish intellectuals and activists. It was rejected by the Arabs who felt that Palestine was an Arab country with a Jewish minority (just like other Arab countries such as Syria, Lebanon, Egypt, Tunisia, or Mo-rocco) and the right of its Arab majority to independent statehood should not be denied or abridged. In the late 1960s, positions were reversed, and it was the Palestinian Arabs who espoused the binational idea, which in turn became unacceptable to Jews, who had by then estab-lished the Jewish state of Israel in most of historic Palestine. In the late 1960s, the Palestine National Council, the legislative arm of the PLO, adopted a political program calling for the resolution of the Arab-Jewish conflict by establishing Palestine as a "democratic secular state" in which Muslim, Christian, and Jewish inhabitants shared equal rights and responsibilities. The PLO continued to call for this solution to the conflict, which in his speech to the UN General Assembly in 1974 PLO leader Yasir Arafat called the Palestinian Dream, until it responded to an emerging world consensus in favor of partition and the two-state solution, which the PLO adopted in 1974.

After a series of Arab-Israeli wars, a legacy of suffering and bitter-ness came to characterize Arab-Jewish relations, giving rise to a widely disseminated myth, belied by real history, that Arabs and Jews have been antagonists since time immemorial. In fact, historically, Arabs and Jews have been closer to each other than they have been to any other peoples in the world. Arab-Jewish enmity is a recent intrusion and a colossal distortion of a long historic legacy of the two peoples. But somehow the myth seems unfortunately to prevail over the fact, and it has become unacceptable to believe in the possibility of Arab-Jewish coexistence beyond the wary coexistence of separate states. Hence the popularity of the two-state solution at the expense of the more humanistic binational solution.

The binational solution to the Palestinian-Israeli conflict is not only ideologically superior to partition and the two-state solution, in the sense that it is based on the principle of the brotherhood of man and the more progressive notion of pluralist community, but also more satisfying to the needs and aspirations of both peoples. It enlarges the geographic limits within which the citizens of the state may wish to live to satisfy their emotional, religious,or economic needs, and it deepens the interdependence of the two peoples to make future conflict mutually harmful and therefore less likely. It facilitates the integration of the Jewish community in the Holy Land in the larger Middle Eastern community, and it makes it more difficult to isolate them than if they had isolated themselves into a separate and distinct Jewish state within a regional non-Jewish environment. Being an integral part of a binational community, they are less likely to be perceived as intruders to the degree that a Jewish state is bound to be perceived in a predominantly Arab-Islamic regional environment. Within the context of a shared homeland, Palestinians and Israelis have the opportunity to blend the Arab and Jewish genius to create in the Holy Land a model for the rest of the region.

Most important, the binational republic would go farther than any other solution to the conflict in responding to the claims to the land which both Arabs and Jews harbor, because the reunification of the Holy Land as a common homeland would in fact fulfill these claims for both peoples. Nothing else, and certainly not partition, would do so. In fact, the only shortcoming of the binational scenario is its lack of political acceptability at this stage in the history of Arab-Jewish relations. But there is nothing immutable about these relations and they are bound to evolve and change. And here is where the historic role of partition and the two-state solution, as a transitional solution, lies. The two-state solution would quiet the raging nationalisms of the two peoples and diminish their mutual fears (Israel's fear for its survival and Palestinian fear of national denial). Partition and the two-state solution would help the parties become gradually accustomed to the shift from strife to coexistence, first in separate states and then in a shared homeland. With time, the unthinkable becomes thinkable and perhaps even desirable and inevitable.

This is not an argument against the ongoing peace process, and it is not a warning of its likely consequences. But it is an argument against the premise that its results should be enshrined as the ultimate wisdom on the future of Israel and Palestine. Palestinian and Israeli nationalisms, which require as a transitional measure the creation of separate Arab and Jewish states in the Holy Land, should some day be elevated to Arab-Jewish humanism to be expressed in a more imaginative and nobler form of coexistence than is possible at the present. But the imperatives of the present must never be assumed to be the limits of the future and its promise.

11

Christianity and the Future of Israeli-Palestinian Relations

by Rosemary Radford Ruether

The discussion of the relation of Christianity to the future of Israeli-Palestinian relations needs to encompass several communities of Christians who have very different relationships to Israel-Palestine. There are the Arab Palestinian Christian communities in historic Palestine, either in Israel or in the Occupied Territories, who have been steadily dwindling since the beginning of Zionist settlement and are in danger of becoming so small that they have little impact on intra-Palestinian or inter-religious relations. There is also the Christian component within the Palestinian diaspora who, however, generally choose to speak as Palestinians, not as Christians. Then there are the Western Christians of Europe and North America who are often oblivious to the existence of Palestinian Christians and focus what scant interest they have in the region on their relations to Jews and Israel.

Before considering the very different viewpoints of Palestinian and Western Christians to Israeli-Palestinian relations, I wish to begin by surveying the developments in these relations through the so-called peace process since 1993. Palestinians today generally regard this peace process as a snare and a delusion by which Israel is seeking to legally consolidate its conquest of almost all of historic Palestine and the final marginalization of the Palestinian people.

This view is shared by many critical Arab and Western scholars and commentators on the region, such as Hisham Sharabi (professor of Arab culture, Georgetown University), Norman Finkelstein (professor of political science, New York University), Salim Tamari (professor of sociology, Birzeit University), Haidar Abdel Shafi (chairman of the Palestinian delegation at the Madrid talks of 1991-2), Simona Sharoni (professor of peace and conflict resolution studies, American University), and others who met to discuss Oslo's Final Status and the Future of the Middle East in July 1997, under the auspices of the Center for Policy Analysis on Palestine.

Norman Finkelstein's paper, "Oslo: Last Stage of Conquest," made a particularly trenchant analysis of the meaning of Oslo. According to Finkelstein, the Zionist project, despite its distinctive features related to Jewish "return," falls into the general trajectory of colonialist conquest of another people's land while seeking to either remove or subjugate the people of that land. Like other Western colonialist projects (including the Euro-American conquest of the Americas) Zionism simultaneously mythologized the land as "empty" and hence "open" for the taking (expressed in the phrase "a people without land for a land without people"), and viewed the indigenous people as subhuman and therefore not fit candidates for human rights.

However, because the Zionist project came late in the Western colonialist trajectory, when Latin Americans, Asians, and Africans were throwing off colonial rule and asserting their human and civil rights, the mass extermination of natives that had been typical of European and Euro-American treatment of American Indians and Africans in the sixteenth through the nineteenth centuries was no longer acceptable in international politics. Hence Zionism from the 1930s through the 1950s hit on a second way of clearing the land of Palestinians in order to make it available for Jewish settlers: expulsion or transfer. Although selected massacres did take place, such as that at Deir Yassin in April of 1948 by the Irgun soldiers and the forced march of the populace of Lydda by Moshe Dayan in July 1948, these killings were part of a strategy of expulsion. They were intended to terrorize Palestinians into fleeing from the area or, failing that, forcibly expelling them.

As a result of this policy, carried on mostly under the cover of war in 1947-9, about a million Palestinians were cleared from the expanded territory that became the de facto borders of Israel in 1950. The United Nations partition plan of 1947 had allotted 55 percent of Palestine, on the coast, the eastern Gaza, the Negev, and eastern Galilee, for a Jewish state, even though there were only 600,000 Jews in this region owning only seven percent of the land and this area contained an equal number of Palestinians. The other 45 percent was allotted for a Palestinian Arab state where about a million Palestinians lived.

In 1947-9, under cover of war, the Jewish army seized another 20 percent of the land, Jordan occupied the West Bank and East Jerusalem, and Egypt took over the Gaza Strip. A remnant of about 160,000 Palestinians remained within the expanded Jewish borders; these had mostly become landless. Only about ten percent of the land remained in Palestinian hands (this has been steadily eroded in subsequent years) while 90 percent of the land (since expanded) fell under Jewish collective ownership. The territory allotted for the Palestinian state disappeared, partitioned between an expanded Jewish state (42 percent) and Jordanian and Egyptian occupation (48 percent). The expelled Palestinians became refugees in the West Bank and Gaza and the surrounding Arab states.

Thus this first project of expulsion, clearing the land for Jewish settlement, seemed to be a resounding success. However, the problem of Palestinian presence for the Zionist project has continued. The Palestinian remnant in Israel has grown to 1,163,000 today. In 1967, Israel conquered the remaining Palestinian areas of the Gaza Strip and West Bank. Palestinians in those regions today number about 2,750,000. Jews in Israel face a Palestinian population moving toward the 4 million mark, while Jews, despite enormous efforts to import settlers, especially from Russia, are 4.7 million. Thus the "demographic problem" (i.e., Palestinians insufficiently reduced to a landless, insignificant minority) has not been "solved."

While expulsion was covered up and denied in 1947-9 and was carried out without Western protest, this could not happen under the greater glare of visibility in 1967. Thus shortly after the 1967 conquest and occupation of the West Bank and Gaza, military and Labor Party leaders conceived of a new plan to render this population insignificant, which Finkelstein calls "encirclement." This was the Allon Plan of 1967. This plan called for the building of a ring of settlements around Jerusalem and the annexation of this area into Israel. In addition, a line of settlements would be placed down the Jordan Valley. Land around these settlements would be expanded, while the Palestinian population would be reduced to largely landless enclaves in major population centers. This would eventually lead to a new partition of the West Bank and Gaza Strip, with the confiscated land taken into Israel, while the Palestinian enclaves would be placed under the government of Jordan.

Other military leaders, such as Moshe Dayan, and, even more, the militant outlook of the settlement movement and the Likud Party, disagreed with even this partial allocation of land to the Palestinians. They hoped to continue to effect, even if by slow but steady measures, the expulsion or forced migration of Palestinians. The Palestinians would become steadily fewer and more landless, those remaining kept under control by military occupation. They would neither be given Israeli citizenship nor autonomous control over any part of the land.

The actual policies of Israel toward the Palestinians in the Occupied Territories over the last 30 years have proceeded on a combination of these two plans. There has been a continual building of settlements around East Jerusalem, first an inner ring and then an outer ring. A gerrymandered territory has been drawn around Arab East Jerusalem which avoids Palestinian population enclaves, while confiscating the agricultural land around them. This settlement ring has now grown to ten times the size of the former East Jerusalem, reaching beyond Ramallah to the north, almost to Jericho in the east and beyond Bethlehem to the south, with the first ring annexed into Israel.

In addition, settlements have been expanded in the West Bank and Gaza, as well as land taken for public purposes such as military use and roads for Jewish settlers. The result is that Israel has confiscated about 70 percent of the West Bank and 40 percent of Gaza. The Palestinians within these regions have been denied the right to expand or build new houses, and are subject to a continual effort to withdraw their residency permits in Jerusalem. A network of bypass roads have been and continues to be built, confiscating more Palestinian land, linking Jewish settlements with each other, but, through continual closures and denial of travel permits, cutting Palestinians in the enclaves off from each other and from Jerusalem. Thus, Palestinians have been ever more ghettoized in separate enclaves with few economic or cultural resources.

In 1987, Palestinians rose in protest against these repressive policies and organized a combination of street protests, boycotts, and efforts to organize committees of economic and cultural survival and development. Despite violent repression in which some 2,000 people died and 150,000 were injured, many permanently, and hundreds of thousands detained (and tortured) in prison, this uprising (intifada) continued until 1993. Sympathy and concern for a just settlement grew among Western nations, usually defined in terms of a two-state solution in which Palestinians would be granted an independent state in the West Bank and Gaza (now 20 percent of historic Palestine, not the 45 percent given them by the United Nations in 1947).

Despite protests by more militant Palestinian groups (who continued to hope for a return of all of historic Palestine or at least a right of return to towns now in Israel from which they had been expelled), in 1988 the PLO, led by Yasir Arafat, accepted a historic compromise. They declared that they recognized the existence of the state of Israel in its 1967 borders, contingent on a return of the land taken in 1967 for an independent Palestinian state with its capital in East Jerusalem.

Recognizing the growing post-Gulf War international pressure for a settlement that would concede some kind of Palestinian entity, Labor leaders Yitzhak Rabin and Shimon Peres hit on a brilliant plan. They would agree to a peace process that would give some autonomous regions to Palestinian control, but in a way that would actually consolidate and legalize the settlements around East Jerusalem, the West Bank, and Gaza. This would amount to a new partition of the remnant of Palestine, along the lines conceived 25 years earlier in the Allon plan. Enclaves of Palestinian population would be given local self-government, but not real sovereignty, separated from the territories of Israeli settlement, which would be annexed into Israel.

What was lacking for this plan in the past had been the presence of a Palestinian national leadership that could be entrusted with local Palestinian self-government as effective "native police" under Israel, to enforce Palestinian compliance on a day-to-day basis. This idea of creating a puppet Palestinian police, billed as Palestinian self-government, had been tried in 1975 in the form of the village leagues. But these failed due to the refusal of Palestinians in these towns and villages to accord these "collaborators" the status of legitimate representatives. It was here that Rabin and Peres hit on their most ingenious plan. This was to coopt a corrupt and declining PLO leadership under Yasir Arafat to play the role of leader of a collaborator local police.

Arafat and the PLO had been vehemently demonized by Israel. All dialogue of Israelis with their representatives was made illegal. But Rabin and Peres were well aware that Arafat had not only declared his acceptance of the "historic compromise" of a mini-Palestinian state in the West Bank and Gaza, but said he would be willing to begin with any territory, no matter how small, that was conceded by Israel as a base for this state. Only Arafat and the PLO under him had the status of legitimate national leadership for Palestinians as a whole. A dramatic turnabout to dialogue and negotiation with the PLO under Arafat, allowing him and his guerrilla fighters to return to be the recipients of territory turned over to a Palestinian local administration, appeared to be a startling concession by Israel.

In the Oslo plan it was agreed that the densely populated Palestinians areas, the Gaza Strip, Jericho, Ramallah, Bethlehem, Nablus, Tulkarem, and Hebron, would be turned over to a Palestinian National Authority. Arafat and his PLO fighters would be transformed into this Authority. The hope was held out of a larger process in which the final status of East Jerusalem, additional land, and the return of refugees would be resolved, leading to an eventual Palestinian sovereign state in all or most of the West Bank and Gaza.

The world was amazed and rejoiced at what was billed as a historic turnabout and "conversion" of these old enemies to "peace." In 1993, President Bill Clinton staged the historic handshake of Rabin and Arafat on the White House lawn. But it soon became clear to Palestinians (but not to Westerners committed to a rosy view of this peace process) that what the Labor leaders really had in mind was not a process that would eventually lead to an independent Palestinian state in all or even most of the West Bank and Gaza, with Jerusalem as its capital, but rather a version of the old Allon and Village League plans in new disguise.

The peace process turned out to be based on a division of the West Bank and Gaza into three zones. Area A, the densely populated Palestinian enclaves, would be turned over to the Palestinian authority. These together are about six percent of the West Bank and Gaza Area C (Israeli settlements) would remain under Israeli control. Intermediate areas (Palestinian agricultural land that was disputed and not yet settled by Israelis, including water resources) would be negotiated between the two authorities, but it appears unlikely that Palestinians will receive much of it.

Moreover, in the period between the first stage and the final stage of the peace process, Israel, far from refraining from further settlements, engaged in a rush to consolidate as much land in the West Bank and Gaza under exclusive Jewish control as possible. There was stepped-up settlement around Jerusalem. There was feverish road building, linking Jewish areas, by-passing and cutting off Palestinian areas. There were intensified efforts to clear Palestinians from East Jerusalem and its expanded areas through denial of residency permits and destruction of houses deemed to have been constructed "illegally."

It became even more difficult for Palestinians to get permits to travel into and through Jerusalem, cutting off both employment in Israel and communication between Palestinian regions. Continual closures sealed these Palestinians off totally from one another and Israel. Soon militant Palestinians responded with new protests, suicide bombing in the streets of West Jerusalem, killing dozens of Israelis. But each such incident became a new rationale for total closures and sealings of the Palestinian areas, new land confiscation and settlements, new demolition of Palestinian homes. Moreover, although the Israeli army had withdrawn from the centers of Palestinian population, they remained as the enforcers of the walls of enclosure around them. Each incident was used to pressure the Palestinian Authority to be the police agents of repression of dissent (especially of members of the militant Hamas movement), even though there was little evidence that most of the local Hamas members and PLO critics arrested had direct links to the bombers. If Arafat did not do a good enough job at repression of his own people, money for the Palestinian Authority was withdrawn, with the final threat being a reincursion of the Israeli army into the Palestinian enclaves to enforce this repression directly.

Little of the money given to Arafat or the Palestinian Authority was used for development that gave new jobs or cultural institutions to Palestinians. It became clear that this money was to be used primarily for police and security repression. In the five years from the beginning of the peace process to 1997, Palestinians grew rapidly even more impoverished, losing 36 percent of their already miserable GNP (the equivalent of $6 billion), while a corrupt PLO leadership flaunted large houses and cars and were surrounded by bodyguards.

It became evident that the real meaning of the peace process was entrapment in an apartheid system that enclosed Palestinians in their ghettos, denying them the possibility of real autonomous development. Yet there seemed to be no way to legitimately regain a voice to protest this trap or to define an alternative that could be heard by the international community. The ultimate genius of the Israeli peace process was to deny Palestinians not only their land, but their voice as well.

In 1995, Yitzhak Rabin was gunned down by a militant Jewish fundamentalist who saw him as having betrayed the absolute claims of Jews to all the land by "giving away" land to the Palestinians and making peace with Israel's enemies. Subsequently the Labor Party, led by Shimon Peres, was defeated and Benjamin Netanyahu of the Likud Party became prime minister. These dramatic events made it easy for Western liberals to cast Rabin as the hero-martyr of peace who sought a just coexistence with the Palestinians, while Netanyahu was seen as representing an intransigent effort to scuttle the peace process.

But this radical distinction between Rabin and Netanyahu, between Labor and Likud, is misleading. All the policies of encirclement and slow expulsion of the Palestinians outlined above were crafted by the Labor Party, who also led the 1947-9 expulsion of a million Palestinians and the destruction of over 400 villages, and the policy of shootings and breaking of bones that led to so many deaths and permanent injuries during the intifada.

The major difference between Labor and Likud in relation to Palestinian rights is rhetorical. Labor is oriented more to the Western liberal audience and so they shape their public relations in a way that enunciate reasonable and humane perspectives, while carrying out a ruthless policy of steady creation of facts on the ground; i.e., take-over of land, removal or marginalization of Palestinians. Likud is oriented to the religious and conservative parties in Israel that believe in principle in take over of land and removal of Palestinians. Thus it voices these views more forthrightly, but the actual policies presently being pursued by Netanyahu are substantially the same as those shaped by Rabin. Netanyahu's public statements allow Westerners to see more truthfully what is actually going on, but they are misled in constructing this as a dualism of fair Labor and unfair Likud.

The Christian community, both the Palestinian Christians and Western Christians in communication with them, could play a vital role in helping regain a legitimate voice of protest for the Palestinians and a quest for genuine alternatives. But this mediating role has been largely blocked by the acceptance by of most Western Christians of the "peace process," fueled by a desire to think the best of Israeli "good will," and a readiness to stereotype Palestinians as terrorists, now made even worse as "Islamic terrorists."

Christians of Western Europe and North America fall into two major lines of thought toward Israeli-Palestinian relations, or more appropriately, toward Israel, since Palestinians are seldom thought about at all in either view. A small but militant and influential group, associated with more fundamentalist forms of Protestant Christianity, are Christian Zionists. A larger but more diffuse group of Western Christians share some Christian Zionist views, but their main perspective is shaped by a desire to compensate for past Christian anti-Semitism by affirming positive ecumenical relations with Jews.

The basic tenets of the Christian Zionist view interconnect the following propositions: 1) God gave the Jews all of the land of Palestine as a promised land in Biblical times, and this divine donation of land gives Jews today a permanent and unconditional right to occupy all of this land, regardless of other people who have been living there historically (i.e., the Palestinians); 2) as preparation for the events that will culminate world history, all the Jewish people must return to the land, resettle all of it, and rebuild the temple; and 3) the founding of the state of Israel and Jewish settlement of the land are fulfillments of Biblical prophecy which will usher in the final days of judgment and redemption. This will be completed when the Jews are converted to (evangelical Protestant) Christianity. The battle of Armageddon will then take place, killing the enemies of God (unbelievers, Communists, Muslims). The saints (including the converted Jewish elect) will be raptured to heaven while God cleanses the earth of evil doers. Then these saints will descend to a purified earth to enjoy millennial blessings.

This extraordinary ideology, while ultimately anti-Jewish and genocidal, places these fundamentalist Christians on the side of the most militant of Jewish fundamentalist settlers who desire to settle all the land, expel all Palestinians, and destroy the Muslim holy buildings on the Temple Mount in order to rebuild the temple, founding a strictly observant Torah state.

While most Western Christians, including evangelicals, do not believe this whole scenario literally, aspects of it, particularly versions of the ideas that Jews have a God-given right to the land that supercedes the rights of Palestinians and that Israel should be seen as a "special" (redemptive, holy, or exemplary) state, are widely held even by liberal Christians. These notions of the God-given right of Jews to the land and the special status of Israel are joined in the minds of these liberal Christians with feeling of guilt for the Holocaust and/or some need to compensate for past anti-Semitism by affirming "good" ecumenical relations with Jews.

While these sentiments that Christians should repent of past anti-Semitism and cultivate a positive relation with Jews and Judaism are appropriate in themselves, unfortunately they have been construed primarily as a Christian duty of uncritical support for the state of Israel. This means that mention of the Palestinian plight is ignored altogether. Most such Christians avoid learning anything about the Palestinians. It is implicitly assumed that any concern for injustice to Palestinians, indeed any discussion of Palestinians at all, is anti-Semitic. So such Christians evade knowing and hence having to speak about them in order not to be denounced as anti-Semitic by those Jews with whom they wish to cultivate "ecumenical relations."

Christian repentance for the Holocaust and anti-Semitism have been effectively distorted into a silencing of Western Christians in regard to Palestinian human and civil rights, a view carefully nurtured and reenforced by the Jewish Zionist establishment in North America especially. Any effort to break through this wall of self-censorship of Western Christians in regard to injustices to Palestinians by those seeking to communicate an alternative reality is highly frustrating.

When I have tried to talk about this to Christian audiences of the type that seek to be "ecumenical" toward Jews, I typically encounter a range of responses. On one end of the spectrum are those who say frankly, "Well, I know that bad things are going on, but I just don't dare to speak about it publicly. I don't want to be vilified by Jews." There are others who ask helplessly, "How can the Jews do this, when they themselves were oppressed?" At the other end of the spectrum are those who openly claim that any such discussion is anti-Semitic or at the least one should not speak about it as Christians "because of the Holocaust."

It seems impossible to communicate to any of these Christians that there might be some way of being concerned about justice for Palestinians that would also be an expression of positive regard for Jews as well. The notion that Christians can only have good relations with Jews by turning a blind eye to the plight of Palestinians seems unshakable. Palestinians are made to pay for the sins of Western Christians against the Jews.

It will not be possible to break this wall of silence toward Palestinians until Western Christians recognize what it is that they are doing when they construct this wall. There is a need to understand, not only what is happening to Palestinians in Israel and the Occupied Territories, but also our own role, as European and American Christians, in the promotion of the ethnocide of the Palestinian people. In effect it is Western Christians, especially British and American, who created and continue to create the historical framework in which this process of ethnocide goes on.

Moreover we have done it and continue to do it in the name of reconciliation with Jews. It is Americans particularly who provide the money and arms through our government that allows this to happen. But Western Christians generally have created the historical ideology that legitimizes this process. We legitimize it as something that is "due" to Jews, both from Biblical land claims, but also as compensation for our past guilt. This legitimization is then reinforced by the wall of silence around the resulting injustice to the Palestinians that prevents this from being seen, heard, and understood. By doing this, we seek to salve our bad conscience for our past genocide of European Jews.

Why are Western Christians so unable to recognize what they are doing? Why is injustice to Palestinians so invisible or unimportant to them? Why do they imagine they are rectifying a injustice to one people, the Jews, that took place in the totally different historic context of Europe, by keeping silence about the ongoing destruction of another people, the Palestinians? Perhaps part of the problem is that Christians still do not accept Jews as ordinary human beings. We still need to construct them in some archetypal scheme as paradigms of either exemplary virtue or exemplary vice.

Seeking to escape from the evil consequences of making Jews the paradigms of vice, we flip to the opposite pole of seeing Jews as incapable of wrong, paragons of folk wisdom, and founders of a messianic state. To recognize that great evil is being done by Israeli Jews to Palestinians in the construction of this state makes us feel anxious that we are falling back to the other pole of the dualism; i.e., Jews as preternaturally evil. Jews are not allowed to be ordinary people, with a range of capacities, good and bad, in different contexts of power and powerlessness. This myopia is bad enough in personal relations, but fatal in world politics.

My guess is that Western Christians cannot break out of this myopia by themselves, because its contradictions are too invisible to them. It is only through corrective experiences, especially experiences with the Palestinian people in their own homeland, that they can come face-to-face with the alternative realities that can shatter their self-enclosed framework and open up a different approach. Palestinian Christians are key mediators here to both introduce Western Christians to the Palestinian reality, but also to correct the misuse of Christian symbols, such as repentance, promised land, and Jewish-Christian ecumenical relations that have been misconstrued from the Western Christian perspective.

Here Palestinian liberation and contextual theologies can play a key role. Palestinian Christian theologians, such as Naim Ateek and Mitri Raheb, have been shaping a Palestinian theology both to shatter this distorted use of Christianity to justify Israeli colonialism, and also to enunciate a positive theology of just coexistence of Jewish and Palestinian people in the homeland they both love and wish to claim.

Palestinian liberation theology rests on two major theses. The first and most important of these has to do with the nature of God, and our relation to God, and the second our relation to our neighbor, in the context of relations between two peoples, Israelis and Palestinians, and three religions, Judaism, Christianity, and Islam in the one land of Israel/Palestine.

For Palestinian Christians, the question raised by Jewish and Christian Zionist use of Scripture to justify exclusive land claims is not God's existence, but God's nature. Palestinian Christians assume that God exists, but the disturbing question is "what kind of God exists?" Is it a God of war and vengeance, a tribal God who chooses one people, the Jews, at the expense of another people, the Palestinians? For Palestinian theologians, the true God is a God of justice, truth and peace for all peoples, a God who calls all peoples into relations of justice and peace with each other. A tribal God who chooses one people against another is a nationalist idol, not the true God.

Ateek does not see this distinction as setting Christianity against Judaism. He would distinguish two traditions in Hebrew Scripture. One is a tribalistic tradition that sees God as electing the Jews in an ethnically exclusive way, permitting violent rejection of the other peoples of the land. But there is also the prophetic tradition that criticizes the tribal tradition and moves toward a vision of the God of justice for all people. Ateek sees Jesus and authentic Christianity as rooted in the prophetic universalist tradition of the Bible, but also acknowledges that Christians can revert to the tribal God, as has been the case with various kinds of Christian nationalism and Christian Zionism.

Both communities need to renew the prophetic universalistic traditions of their faith against tendencies to fall into nationalist and militarist patterns of religion. This will also mean that Christians overcome exclusivist views of Christianity vis-a-vis Jews (and Muslims). We need to find a way to affirm a God of justice for all people who calls us into mutually affirming coexistence, against exclusivist views that identify the oneness of God with the unique election of one religious group against others. It is this false identification of the oneness of God with favoritism to one people that creates theologies that justify violence and oppression. Only an understanding of God that loves and commands justice for all peoples equally can create the framework for just coexistence of the two people, Israelis and Palestinians, and the three religions, Judaism, Christianity, and Islam, calling them to be equal partners, brothers and sisters, in sharing together the one land they love in justice and peace.

Palestinian liberation theology thus provides for the Western Christian a critical understanding to liberate them both from their own anti-Semitic exclusivism against Jews and also their compensatory partiality that assumes they can only repent of anti-Semitism by special favoritism of Jews and Israel at the expense of Palestinians. It opens up a framework for a Christian advocacy of just peace for both people in their three religions with one another.

The realities of injustice of Jews toward Palestinians, as well as Christian or Islamic ideological exclusivism and violence against Jews, are not covered up, but exposed and confronted. Only by truthful critique of all ideologies that justify oppression can there be a hope for a just sharing of the land and hence true peace. Jews, Christians, and Muslims, Israelis and Palestinians, committed to this goal can join hands as friends in an authentic ecumenism.

12

A Vision for the Palestinian Future

by Souad Dajani

This is an essay about vision, how Palestinians can look toward their future beyond "Oslo." It is not primarily about strategy, and does not, therefore, chart a course of action. It looks at the aftermath of "Oslo," where instead of living in their long-sought for independent state, Palestinians remain refugees and exiles outside of their homeland and a dominated people within. In this essay, I argue that events have come full circle since the early days of Jewish settlement in Palestine. Today, once again, both Palestinians and Israeli Jews find themselves locked in a struggle for the soul and identity of Palestine/Israel. This essay is about the historical events and developments that have brought us where we are, the strategic miscalculations and missteps that may have cost us two states, and the elements of a new vision for the future.

This is an essay, ultimately, about truth and power, and the power of truth. It is about the power of truth embodied in the words of Czech Republic President Vaclav Havel, "living the truth," and in Gandhi's *satyagraha*, "truth with power." It is the truth and power echoed in the phrase, "No fist is big enough to hide the sky," the idea that truth cannot be hidden forever, that so powerfully captured the struggle of the people of Guinea Bissau and Cape Verde against Portuguese colonial rule. It is about the interplay and dialectics between social reality and social consciousness, and about how oppressed peoples can prevail over their oppressors.

What is truth here? That Palestinians do exist, that their expulsion from their homeland was real, and that their national claims are just and legitimate, and have not been achieved.

What about power? It is recognized that "power" is located and institutionalized in social structures. These structures become entrenched, and challenges to them amount to challenges to those vested interests served through such structures. Hence they are very resistant to change. Yet, in the U.S., when Blacks launched the Civil Rights Movement, they were not deterred by the apparent immutability of "white" social arrangements. Nor did Black South Africans cease their struggle against apartheid until they succeeded in abolishing it. Examples such as these illustrate two powerful forces at work: they prove that social structures are not inviolable; over time, those who are subordinated and oppressed by these structures can and do become conscious of their oppression and rise against it. And, these examples show that social movements can and do amass a following, where people are carried along by a vision of a better future to replace the past. Such visions are especially powerful and compelling when they include and encompass, rather than exclude and marginalize, the former oppressors. In their ideal form, such visions point the way to a more equal, just, and humanistic future for all.

What is the power Palestinians can wield? Answering this question needs to acknowledge the asymmetry in power between Israel and the Palestinians, occupiers and occupied, but insists that Palestinians possess a different, yet significant, source of power.

What is that power? Though Palestinians cannot defeat Israel militarily, nor can they capture or defend geographical territory as such, they can put to good use the kind of power they wielded so effectively during the intifada, the kind of power that placed their national cause onto the world stage: they can attempt to defeat Israel's political will.

Israel's political will has taken different thrusts over the years, from the early and ongoing Zionist attempts to erase the Palestinian cause from the historical record and replace it with a Zionist narrative of "making the desert bloom," "a land without people for a people without land," and so on. Israel has also imposed its political will through its occupation of Palestinian lands and its repression, often brutal, of Palestinians in the Occupied West Bank and Gaza Strip. Israel has tried to crush the Palestine Liberation Organization (PLO) — the representative, voice, and symbol of the existence of the Palestinian national cause — by invading Lebanon in 1982 and laying siege to Beirut. Israel has used its main ally, the U.S., to evade its obligations under UN resolutions. Finally, Israel has sought to use "negotiations" with Palestinians, from the time of the launching of the Madrid Conference in October 1991, to the signing of the Declaration of Principles in 1993 and the other accords since then, to bypass the political issue of occupation and solidify Israeli-Jewish claims to all the area of Palestine. In this scenario, Palestinian "nationalism" would be permanently precluded in exchange for limited civil and political rights in areas of "self-rule."

But Palestinians have stubbornly refused to go away or to resign themselves to such a fate. Living in proximity to Jews in the whole area of Israel/Palestine, just as in the early days of the British Mandate over Palestine, Palestinians have a unique opportunity to reassert their truth, wield their power, and significantly, hold up to Israel the image of a more dignified and just future than any previously offered — or realized — by Zionism. As I argue below, once dismissed as "unthinkable," this vision would necessarily encompass both peoples, and would best be expressed in the form of a binational state. This is the vision, supported by truth, and power, that is the topic of this essay.

As we inched toward the end of 1997, the fifth year since the signing of the Declaration of Principles (DOP) between Israel and the PLO in 1993, peace never seemed more remote. Provisions in the DOP for "interim" stages had not been fulfilled. More troubling, in the eyes of Palestinians, was that hopes for resolving "final status" issues by creating an independent Palestinian state in the West Bank and Gaza Strip, appeared increasingly unlikely.

The year 1997, also marked several "anniversaries." Sadly, for Palestinians, none were cause for celebration. It marked the 80th year since the issuing of the Balfour Declaration in 1917. This declaration called for the establishment of a "Jewish homeland" in Palestine, so long as nothing was done to prejudice the "civil and religious rights of the non-Jewish population" (who then amounted to some 93 percent of the total population of Palestine). Fifty years ago, in November 1947, the United Nations General Assembly (UNGA) voted on Resolution 181, by virtue of which Palestine would be partitioned into two states and Jerusalem would be internationalized. The Jewish state was allotted 55 percent of the most fertile and productive lands, while the Palestinians, who then still constituted a demographic majority, were given the remaining 45 percent. Yet, within two short years, Palestine was essentially vacated of its indigenous Arab inhabitants, as Arabs fled or were forcibly expelled by Zionist Jewish forces. Thirty years ago, in 1967, the remaining areas of Mandate Palestine that had not become part of the state of Israel in 1948, were captured. This placed the West Bank, the Gaza Strip, and East Jerusalem under an Israeli occupation that has persisted since. Ten years ago, in 1987, Palestinians in these areas launched their intifada, the popular uprising that symbolized Palestinian rejection of Israeli rule and their struggle to end the occupation. Instead of liberation, however, Palestinians found themselves, five years after the signing of the DOP, still under Israeli control, a situation that was complicated by the installation of a Palestine Authority, whose own responsibilities under the DOP and subsequent accords seemed to facilitate, entrench, and preserve this Israeli rule.

Ironically, it was "Oslo" (the generic term for the various accords), that brought us, as Israeli Jews and Palestinian Arabs, full circle to where we began. By precluding the establishment of a separate and independent Palestinian state in the Occupied Territories, by enabling Israel not only to retain overall control of these areas (land, security, resources, settlements, borders, the "Greater Jerusalem," and the like), but to accelerate its pace of road and settlement building to serve Jews only; the "Green Line" that supposedly distinguished Israel proper from the territories it occupied in 1967, was effectively erased.

The days in which a two-state solution may have been both possible and feasible, had apparently passed — ironically too, because of Israel's own refusal to countenance such a solution at the appropriate time. With a "Green Line" increasingly crisscrossed by roads and settlements, with an Arab population inside Israel that comprised close to 20 percent of Israeli citizens, with a 94 percent Palestinian Arab population in the West Bank and Gaza Strip under the ultimate control of the Israeli Ministry of Defense, with the close parity between Arab and Jewish populations in the Greater Jerusalem area, only two scenarios were at hand: either apartheid, or binationalism. A solution based on Palestinian "entities," with nominal autonomy, would never be a basis for a permanent peace, not least because it side-stepped the historical injustice committed against the Palestinian people.

Over the years of conflict, Palestinians, as well as some Israeli Jews, had been willing to reach an accommodation — one that would have offered two states for two peoples, in lieu of the single homeland/state belonging to all, or claimed exclusively by one people. The notion of two states was premised on international law, including UN Security Council Resolution 242 of November 1967, that underscored the "inadmissibility" of territory captured through war, and that called upon Israel to withdraw from the territories it captured in June 1967. The two-state option was also supported by other UN resolutions that called for "self-determination" for the Palestinian people. However, this solution remained, for many, an imperfect one. For Palestinians, it would have meant putting aside forever the very idea of their homeland, and permanently relinquishing claims for a return to their homes and lands. For Israeli Jews, especially those to whom the West Bank and Gaza Strip were part of the "Jewish homeland," the thought of giving up these territories was anathema.

But "Oslo" did not address itself to history nor to the essence of the conflict, which boils down to lands, legitimacy, and identity — and the asymmetry in power between Israel and the Palestinians. The Oslo Accords had nothing to say about the legitimate rights of Palestinians to national independence, nor about the millions of Palestinians, refugees and others, who waited or languished outside of Palestine, longing for home, security, a normal life, and an end to their exile. By 1997, the accords which were touted at the outset as a "historical breakthrough" in the conflict between Israel and the Palestinians, became transparent in the magnitude of what many perceived as their "betrayal."

Given the lack of redress to the historical injustice committed against Palestinians in these accords, Palestinians who struggled so long for at least a partial redress in the form of two-states, found themselves having to rethink both their strategy and their vision. Despite the intent of the two leaderships, and the U.S. and other players, the very provisions of the accords have caused the fate of the two peoples inhabiting the lands of Israel/Palestine to be ever more closely intertwined. It is in this context that the future must be viewed and planned for. Apartheid, in the form of Palestinian self-rule zones, must be rejected as immoral and untenable. If the two-state option has indeed been foreclosed by developments on the ground, then there is only one solution at hand — binationalism, a shared fate. This is the ground that Palestinians and Jews stand on, to work with or against, but at any rate, one which they cannot ignore.

The Past

In 1948, my mother was 21 years old, the youngest of seven children. She lived in Jaffa, in a house she shared with her mother, three brothers, and three sisters, on a land rich with orange groves that had been passed down through the family for many generations.

When war broke out in 1948, my mother and her family decided to escape to Tripoli in northern Lebanon, to stay with relatives there and get out of harm's way until the fighting ended and they were able to return home. Anticipating a very short stay, they packed a weekend bag....

The war ended with the declaration of the Jewish state of Israel. My mother and her family were stuck outside, forever barred from returning home. The orange groves passed on to Jewish hands, the house and all its belongings; its books, clothes, antiques, kitchenware, furniture; all the life-possessions of my mother's family, were taken by Jews who were given that house. Until today, the second of my aunts, who is now an 83-year-old widow living in the Gulf, asks me if I can find her the book she was reading when they left Palestine. She says that she left it laying face-down on the nightstand near her bed, and she wanted to know how the book ended. I never found the book, The Five Stepping-Stones. *Neither she nor my mother, nor indeed any of their family, were ever allowed back home.*

Why do I tell this story when every Palestinian has a story to tell? Why relate my own family's history, when other Palestinians experienced even more brutal expulsions, and when so many Palestinians remained refugees, now well into their third or fourth generations, without ever finding a secure home or livelihood elsewhere?

Why do I tell this story now? Because somewhere along the line, Palestinians fell into a defensive and reactive mode. We lost sight of our truth, the unassailable reality of our former existence in Palestine, and we became trapped in the pattern of arguing and debating issues which essentially sidetracked us from our purpose. We reacted to accusations that it was our fault for rejecting UN Resolution 181 in 1947, when the Zionists had accepted it. We debated what if Palestinians had accepted UN Resolution 181? We reacted to accusations that Arabs never wanted peace, and we debated what if Jordan hadn't gone to war in 1967, and what if it hadn't "lost" the West Bank? We reacted to accusations of violence and terrorism, and debated what if Palestinians didn't have the PLO to represent them, what if it had engaged in different tactics, or what if Palestinians in the Occupied Territories hadn't launched their intifada, or had planned it differently? We debated the role and responsibility of Arab states, we debated the role of the U.S., we debated the role of the UN, we debated every single resolution coming out of the Palestine National Council (PNC). Regardless of the question preoccupying us at a given moment, the underlying issue was the same: in each of these instances, we found ourselves on the defensive, unable to take our legitimacy for granted and constantly struggling to reassert it on the world stage. All the while we were trying to counter Zionist propaganda that had gained the initiative (especially in the U.S.) and was succeeding in negating our existence and delegitimizing our history and the reality of our dispossession.

Yet the truth, as my mother's story illustrates, is shocking in its simplicity and veracity. Whatever happened in the decades since 1948 — indeed, since the issuing of the Balfour Declaration in 1917 — the fundamentals remain: Palestinians had their homeland taken away from under them, they were never compensated nor allowed to go home. Instead, in the ensuing years, everything was done, by Jewish Israelis and their supporters, to rewrite that history, to detract from the Palestinian legitimacy, and to make out the victims, the Palestinians, as usurpers and liars. Not only was their homeland physically taken away, but Palestinians like my parents, were robbed of the right to even claim the idea of Palestine. It was as though their lives had never been lived, as though their own existence had been turned into a falsehood.

For a while, it appeared as though Zionism had triumphed. It had succeeded in taking away all the lands of Palestine, and had supplanted its own version of history onto the world stage. Backed by its powerful supporter, the U.S., Israel was also able to evade UN resolutions, and refuse to address the national claims of the Palestinian people. But there was one minor detail: Palestinians did not vanish, nor did they remain passive or silent. Their very existence remained a thorn in Israel's side — for so long as Palestinians were physically present, the question would inevitably be raised, "Who are they and where did they come from if there truly was no such thing as Palestinians in Palestine?" The very fact of their existence would always be a reminder, as Benjamin Beit-Hallahmi called it, of Israel's "original sin." No matter what efforts at damage-control, of physical oppression, of all the measures taken against Palestinians, especially after the 1967 occupation,

Palestinians were not silenced. The intifada, the Palestinian uprising that began in 1987, was a wake-up call to Israel, Palestinians, and the world, that the Palestinian issue could no longer be buried or dismissed. Much of the effort since then to keep some kind of peace process "on track," was, as I argue below, precisely an attempt by Israel and its supporters to buy time and contain the Palestinian issue.

Oslo was simply a culmination of a process that has sought to establish Zionist legitimacy permanently and irrevocably at the total expense of Palestinian legitimacy. Installing a Palestine Authority that basically acceded to the notion that the conflict was not over occupation and national rights, but rather a "dispute" over limited civil and political rights (as a careful reading of the documents reveal) and committing Palestinians to govern the areas on Israel's behalf, only helped to sanctify the presence of the occupation regime over Palestine. Hence the significance of Palestinian capitulation and cooperation with "Oslo."

Expectations of a final and complete victory of Zionism may have been premature, and may have indeed backfired. Though by virtue of these accords Israel found itself possessing all the lands it had coveted, it discovered that it still had to contend with the very Palestinian people it had been trying to escape and ignore. In 1997, the area of Israel/Palestine held close to four million Jews and 3.5 million Arabs, all of whom were determined to stay.

Once again, Jews and Arabs have come full circle, vying for the identity of Palestine. If at one time Israel succeeded in taking away their land and denying their history, Palestinians have before them a unique opportunity to reclaim that history, their truth, their rights. They have the opportunity to hold up a mirror to Israeli Jews, and to other hostile detractors, to show that this time there may be another way. Rather than a single homeland for one people, as Zionists attempted to gain for themselves, or the idea of a single homeland expressed politically in the framework of two states — a choice preferred by Palestinians but never exercised — Palestinians and Israeli Jews can forge together another future, in a binational state that would be the homeland and the state for both peoples. This process has to begin by acknowledging and addressing the Palestinian past, as much as the world has acknowledged and has tried to address the tragic Jewish past in the aftermath of the Holocaust.

This is why my mother's story is important. Because it is part of that history that has been buried and denied, because it is true.

The Present

I was born in Detroit, Michigan in 1953. It seems I was always living an exile within an exile. The first layer was the reality of my parents' exile from Palestine, that in turn caused them to come to the U.S. and seek a life here — the world into which I was born and initially raised. The second layer was caused by the dislocation I experienced, when at age eight, my parents decided to leave the U.S. and settle in Beirut, Lebanon. There I was, a young Arab girl, uprooted from my American ways, and plunged into a seemingly alien Arab culture. The sense of rootlessness, of a foot in two worlds but a foothold in neither, has never left me.

My own defining moment, the turning point in my life, came in 1982, when I was trapped in Beirut during Israel's invasion of Lebanon. It was a powerful and rude awakening.

To say the invasion was a nightmare doesn't begin to capture what it was like. The utter helplessness against Israeli war planes raining death upon us. The attacks, the terror, the destruction were unrelenting.

The invasion "educated" me. Until then, I'd basically bought into the Western ideology of individualism. I thought individuals could challenge their fate, work hard and "make it." Yet, there I was, a young woman, never really politicized, teaching at the American University of Beirut, trying to get a Ph.D., and an American to boot! Did the Israeli planes ever distinguish between me, this somewhat haughty American and some "refugee"? I had been brainwashed too, that somehow Americans had it made, and were, therefore, "deserving." The bombs didn't care. I was no better and no worse than others. I learned that my American passport meant nothing, what mattered was that I am Arab and Palestinian. "Individualism" was only a myth, a divide and rule tactic... I learned.

Why do I tell this story, when thousands of others, both Palestinians and Lebanese suffered infinitely more than I during this invasion? Because, again, it was real, it was truth. Because it was a lesson in how myths are created and believed, as evidenced in my own blind acceptance of Western "values." And because it awoke in me the painful realization that as a Palestinian, I would never have a secure or normal life, nor the hope for one, as long as I shared the same fate with the people whose identity I also shared, the same people who, at any time, could be turned into so arbitrary and casual victims. It was a transformative experience; being put on the edge of survival, the reality of my social existence finally hitting me, and awakening in me the awareness of oppression, of subordination, in a way I had not experienced before. My own awakening paralleled what happened in the Occupied Territories only a few years later, when the whole population rose up en masse during the intifada to shake-off their oppressors.

It was only later that I was able to make the connection and reach the obvious conclusion, that my fate as a Palestinian, indeed the fate of Palestinians as a people, was also bound up with the fate of the Jewish people. Our lives were permanently intertwined. We both needed peace and justice in order to live and thrive. For a while, I, as many other Palestinians, thought this "peace and justice" could best be served by two states for two peoples. And throughout the decades, until the end of the intifada in the early 1990s, I continued to hold onto this view, as did the majority of Palestinians at the time.

The Palestinian intifada first erupted in the Gaza Strip in December 1987. Within a few weeks it had encompassed virtually the whole of the Occupied West Bank and Gaza Strip. While there had been many acts of resistance throughout the years of occupation, the intifada was different. It was distinguished by its pervasiveness throughout the Occupied Territories, and by its largely nonviolent character. Why it was launched at that time and in that form, can only be answered by looking at Israel's occupation of these areas over the preceding 21 years.

Ever since the beginning of the occupation in 1967, Israel instituted policies that were aimed at seizing control of the lands and resources of these areas and integrating them economically into Israel. Israeli policy was also directed at preventing the emergence of any independent Palestinian development. Israeli structures of occupation were cemented and backed by a series of military orders, laws, and regulations that covered virtually every area of daily life. A military administration was immediately put in control of these areas, which remained in force until 1981, when it was nominally replaced by a civilian administration. From then on, the military administration, directly accountable to the Israeli Minister of Defense, retained ultimate responsibility for these areas. In all, well over 1,400 Israeli Military Orders were issued to govern the lives of Palestinians. Often, Israeli laws were supplemented by the use of force, or by the imposition of "collective punishment" against whole communities (imposing curfews, blowing up houses, declaring closed areas, uprooting trees, conducting mass arrests, and the like) — a practice that continued into the Oslo era.

Israel's drive to acquire lands and build Jewish settlements in the Occupied Territories have always been two of the most visible and serious indications of its long-term plans to integrate these areas into Israel. Soon after the June 1967 War, Palestinians were driven from their lands in the tens of thousands, thousands of their homes were destroyed, and several villages were completely eradicated. The Israeli authorities then issued a series of laws and military orders to expropriate large tracts of Arab lands to make way for the establishment of Jewish settlements.

Thousands of dispossessed Palestinians who did not leave, and who, as a consequence of land expropriations lost their means of livelihood, were increasingly forced into cheap wage-labor in the Israeli-dominated economy. This was particularly true in the Gaza Strip, which, as a result of unique historical and structural circumstances, was most severely affected by the Israeli occupation. For both regions, however, dispossession, forced proletarianization, as well as the immediacy of their dependence on Israel, all had a profound impact on Palestinian society, and later prompted Palestinian resistance to occupation.

The roots of the intifada then are clearly located in the realities and structures of occupation, and in what Palestinians perceived as Israeli refusal to reach a political settlement. Palestinians finally decided to take matters into their own hands.

The intifada was largely nonviolent, and it is this characteristic that at once demonstrated the determination of Palestinians to throw off their occupation, and revealed a different way of envisioning a Palestinian and Israeli future. Palestinians were then still struggling for two states, in which they would exercise their rights to national self-determination alongside Israel. By consciously selecting largely nonviolent methods over violent attacks, Palestinians indicated to Israel that they were a serious and trustworthy interlocutor; they were determined to win their independence, yet they did not intend to threaten or destroy Israel. Thus, stone-throwing demonstrations and individual armed attacks against selective Israeli targets notwithstanding, the intifada was deliberately conducted as a universal unarmed civilian struggle against Israeli occupation. Whether conceived as such or not, Palestinians realized it was not "territory" they would be defending against such a powerful opponent. Rather, it was Israel's political will to sustain this occupation that they were challenging.

Palestinians attempted to defeat Israel's political will in various ways: by affecting morale and costs to the army; by splitting Israeli public opinion in ways they hoped would eventually cause ordinary Israelis to realize that the occupation itself was untenable; and by trying to wield direct action so that pressure would be brought to bear on the Israeli government (whether from inside or outside the country) to address the essential political roots of the conflict.

Palestinians learned to wield their power during this uprising with the understanding that they could not overthrow direct structures of oppression and control, but that they could use Israeli power to backfire against itself. By employing different nonviolent tactics, ranging from protests and demonstrations, to actions that established their noncooperation with the Israeli regime, to those that were designed to help build indigenous alternatives to the occupation and serve as an infrastructural basis of a future Palestinian state, they hoped to "force" Israel into realizing that its interests would best be served by reaching an "accommodation" with them — Palestinians — based on two independent and sovereign states.

Though the intifada did have some effect in polarizing Israeli society, this did not result in any significant policy changes, nor in Israel's withdrawal from these areas. Instead, the impact of the intifada seemed to dissipate over the years, as Israel became accustomed to this "low-intensity" warfare (as some Israelis referred to it), and as Palestinians themselves tired and lost their momentum. Palestinians rapidly descended into renewed factionalism and infighting, and escalating their own violent attacks against Israeli civilians, even as Israeli sanctions and repression against them intensified. The final blow to the intifada came with the 1991 Gulf War.

The impact of the Gulf War on Palestinians centered around two areas. First, in the direct impact on their daily lives. When the U.S.-led "international alliance" launched its war to dislodge Iraq from Kuwait, Israel imposed weeks-long curfews on Palestinian areas, with the Gaza Strip suffering the most under an uninterrupted six-week long curfew imposed in January and February 1991. Under these curfews, Palestinians were not only forbidden from going to work or school, they were under virtual collective house arrest, forbidden to leave their homes, even to buy food or seek medical care. The suffering they endured at this time was enormous, a situation not improved by the fact that Israel blamed them for "cheering from the rooftops," as Iraqi Scud missiles landed in Israel, and as Israel (and the U.S.) accused the PLO of "siding with Saddam Hussein." This was the second front on which Palestinians experienced a fallout from the Gulf War.

At the end of this war, whatever successes the intifada had in placing Palestinian national rights in full view of both the Israeli and American publics, were reversed as attempts were made to discredit their cause. Both the U.S. and Israel took full advantage of Arafat's earlier visits with Saddam Hussein to demonstrate that the Palestinian national cause was itself somehow suspect, and Palestinian claims were accordingly illegitimate. The deliberate marginalization of the PLO in the aftermath of the Gulf War left the Palestinians with little choice but to put their trust in the U.S. and participate (initially as a delegation alongside Jordan) in the Madrid Conference. Opened in October 1991, this Conference was designed by the U.S. to "solve" the Arab-Israeli conflict in all its dimensions. However, after dozens of bilateral and multilateral meetings over the next year-and-a-half, the Palestinians and Israel was as far apart as ever on the contours of a settlement. Israel insisted on defining interim stages of "self-rule" without acknowledging itself as an occupier, and without linking interim stages to a final settlement. Palestinians, on the other hand, wanted any agreement on interim self-rule to be clearly linked to a final settlement that would itself be based on the idea of land for peace, and would lead to the establishment of an independent Palestinian state in the West Bank and Gaza Strip. Taking place in fits and starts, these talks were unexpectedly preempted by Oslo.

The "Oslo" era began with signing of the Declaration of Principles (DOP) on September 13, 1993, between Israel and the Palestinians. Since the DOP, four additional agreements have been signed: the Cairo

Agreements of May 4, 1994, that installed interim self-rule in the Gaza Strip and Jericho; the "early empowerment" agreements of August 29, 1994; the Israeli-Palestinian Interim Agreement on the West Bank and Gaza Strip of September 28, 1995, and the Protocol Concerning the Redeployment in Hebron of January 15, 1997.

The special significance of Oslo in light of the long-standing conflict between Israel and the Palestinians is that it introduced a number of qualitative changes to this conflict. The effects of these changes are far-reaching and incalculable in their consequences, and I would argue, in their damage: in essence, it is unprecedented that a people struggling for their right to national liberation should acquiesce, in advance of the removal of that colonization, to the overriding legitimate right of the colonizer to colonize them in the first place. Yet that is what the DOP accomplished. For the first time, Palestinians — the PLO — put their signature to a deal that, for all intents and purposes, delegitimized and invalidated their cause. In one stroke, these accords abolished the notion that the territories of the West Bank and Gaza Strip were "occupied," or that the Palestinians had a national cause that extended beyond the confines of these areas. Instead, it reduced the conflict to one of a dispute between Israel and the Palestinians, one that could be solved by negotiations between the two parties over what limited civil and political rights the Palestinian residents of these areas would eventually enjoy.

Arguably, the signing of the various accords enabled Israel to reach a less costly "accommodation" with the Palestinians than could have been foreseen during the peak of the intifada. The Israeli occupation regime had been left intact, to be administered in part by a Palestinian authority. Israel could reap the benefits of its occupation without incurring the costs of an unwanted domination over another people. The victory of Zionism over Palestinian nationalism seemed complete, a victory that was aided by the position of Israel's closest ally, the United States. The U.S. protected Israel by either tacitly or overtly guaranteeing that Israeli definitions of the situation would prevail. It supported Israel by vetoing UN resolutions critical of Israel. It demanded that the international community keep its hands off the conflict, under the guise that since the two parties had signed these agreements, they should be left to "negotiate" between themselves.

Deliberately overlooked in all this was the striking asymmetry in power between occupier and occupied. The complete body of international law in which the Palestinian cause is enshrined, including all the UN resolutions passed over the last 50 years, could no longer be invoked. With the exception of UN Security Council Resolutions 242 and 338, both the DOP and subsequent accords omit mention of UN resolutions. Even 242 is merely given lip service in the accords. As a careful reading of the provisions of these documents reveal, everything would in fact be done to prevent and preempt the application of this basic resolution. There are no references to other vital UN resolutions such as UNGA 181 that sets the legal foundation for a two-state solution, nor to UNGA 194 of December 1948, that calls for Palestinians to be allowed to return to their homes or be compensated. Instead, the Hebron Protocol, the last in the line of agreements between the two parties (and possibly the last ever to be signed before "final status" issues are decided), omits any reference to 242 altogether. There has been no international outcry at these clear violations of the will of the international community, nor have the Palestinians themselves launched any campaign to alert the world community to the significance of these omissions. Palestinians themselves seem to have acquiesced to the U.S. and Israeli view that these accords naturally and legally supersede any previous rulings.

As the five-year interim stage specified in the DOP neared its end, Palestinians may have lost the last window of opportunity to advance their case before the institutionalization of Oslo became complete. Ironically, and unfortunately, it has taken these five years for the pitfalls of Oslo to be clearly revealed to Palestinians and concerned others. Some observers continued to claim that the problem lay in the intransigence of the Israeli Prime Minister Benjamin Netanyahu, and had Yitzhak Rabin been alive, "peace" would have already been achieved. I for one believe that the problem is not one of personalities, but is a function of the very text and provisions of the accords. These accords were conceived and written in the first place with exclusive Israeli interests in mind. And Israeli interests never once wavered over the years in their adamant rejection of a Palestinian national cause.

On the ground in the Occupied Territories the situation deteriorated. Israel had stalled in the process of transferring additional areas of the West Bank and Gaza Strip to the Palestine Authority (as mandated in the accords), and instead accelerated its settlement-building, and intensified the economic and social strangulation of Palestinian areas. Instead of prospects for a progressively expanding peace, Palestinians found themselves choking under even more restrictive control, this time, under layers of both Palestinian and Israeli authorities.

The effect of the DOP was to blur the lines between inside and outside, between one's opponent and one's own community — friend and foe. The occupation forces had "redeployed" and Palestinian forces replaced Israeli ones. While earlier the West Bank and Gaza Strip were two unmistakably occupied areas, under Oslo, Areas "A," "B," and "C" created a patchwork of territories in both the West Bank and Gaza Strip, designating where Palestinians could enjoy "self-rule," how they could live, how and where they could work, where they could move. The prolonged closure of Palestinian areas first imposed in March 1993, was expanded not only to prevent Palestinians from traveling into East

Jerusalem and Israel, or between the Gaza Strip and the West Bank, but to prevent Palestinians from traveling outside their immediate villages or towns, even to contiguous Palestinian areas. Palestinians found themselves constricted within rapidly shrinking areas, as these "closures" barred their movement and travel, and ripped away their expectations for any normalcy in their daily lives.

For Palestinians, these "facts" on the ground, in advance of negotiations over final status issues, melded with their growing discomfort and concern over Arafat and his rule. For an increasing number of Palestinians, Arafat came to be seen as ineffectual stooge in the hands of Israel, put in place to do its bidding — essentially — to manage the occupation for Israel. Evidence of corruption and abuse of power within the Palestinian Authority (PA), the excessive force and violence employed against Palestinians by security and police forces of the PA, and the inability of Arafat to do more than react to Israeli demands, only heightened such concerns.

Palestinians saw their dream of an independent state vanish before their eyes. Refugees still languished in the camps of Lebanon, Jordan, and elsewhere, forgotten and irrelevant in this "peace process." Inside, the emerging "autonomy," dependent as it was on Israel, was doing better at repressing its own people than advancing the cause of national liberation. Self-rule was becoming nothing more than a euphemistic term designed to mask the substitution of direct Israeli control by an indigenous Palestinian authority. While the majority of the people suffered, this Authority was being ruled by a group of people that enriched itself from its rule.

The Future

Attallah, a Palestinian resident of the village of al-Khader, south of Bethlehem, reflects on the patchwork of areas that circumscribe his life in the West Bank. "My house is in Zone B, my office in the municipal council is in Zone A, and my agricultural land is in Zone C," Attallah points out, laughing. "Why al-Khader was divided into all three zones is a question better addressed to the Palestinian negotiators," he remarks. "All I know is that our negotiators accepted this division." As one young man from al-Khader puts it, the situation gets even more ridiculous. "I have a friend in Beit Sahour whose house itself is divided. The bathroom is in Zone C, and the rest of the house is in Zone A!"

This young man may henceforth need a special permit each time he uses his bathroom. On September 4, 1997, the Israeli Military Commander of "Judea and Samaria" issued a Military Order declaring Areas A and B "closed areas," and determining that, "No person shall enter the closed area and may not reside in it except with a permit from a military commander or whomsoever was appointed by him and in pursuance with the conditions of the permit."

People around the world cried tears of joy as they watched Yitzhak Rabin and Yasir Arafat shake hands on the White House lawn on September 13, 1993. I cried too, but my tears were ones of profound sorrow. I felt betrayed. I felt my parents were betrayed. I felt the memory of Beirut 1982 was betrayed, as was the intifada. "If only" I thought. "If only it were the prelude to a just and lasting peace and a historic reconciliation between the two peoples." Instead, to my mind, it was the end of Palestine, worse, the end of the idea of Palestine. It was a strategic coup for Israel, that in one fell swoop erased the gains of the intifada. I could see the confusion ahead, as the lines between friend and foe blurred, as Palestinians in the territories transferred their focus away from Israel and the occupation, to the excesses of their own leadership. I could see these Palestinians, desperate for succor and hope, latching on to this deal, and in the process, abandoning their own power of resistance. I could see resistance in these areas put off for at least another generation. It would take that long, I thought, for the demarcation lines to become clear once again, for Palestinians to tire of false promises and pacification, and for them to rise against their oppressors.

In lieu of resistance, I predicted violence — unproductive, senseless, aimless violence; violence arising from frustration, from repression, from betrayal. And surely enough, that much has been true. Since the DOP was signed, rates of suicide and attempted suicide have gone up, people fear the "security" forces of the PA for their known cases of abuse and violence. And there is the continuing and deliberate brutalization of Palestinians at the hands of Israeli forces. There is also the violence and terror unleashed by Palestinian suicide bombers, and the dozens of Israeli civilian casualties at their hands. How short-sighted, how misguided, how unnecessary this whole "peace process" appeared, when the intifada had brought us so close to a possible permanent settlement in the form of two states.

Edward Said writes, "We need to remind ourselves that political struggles are always contests of will, in which one side attempts to persuade the other side to give up, to lose the will to resist and fight on. This is not a military but a political and moral matter....

"Unless we mobilize ourselves and our friends, and above all, our voices so that the Zionist project can systematically be shown for what it is and was, we can never expect any change in our status as an inferior and dominated people. Even as Arafat and his men try to unsuccessfully deal with Israel's actions they seem to have forgotten that no voice (voices) speaks for the suffering of the Palestinians, no effort is made to record systematically the wrong we suffer, no energy is expended on trying to organize our various expatriate communities so that they

*can undertake the task of dramatizing and finally defeating the legiti-
macy of the plan to take the whole of Palestine, every significant inch of
our land, every aspect of our past as a people, every possibility of self-
determination in the future. For at bottom our struggle with Zionism
must be won first on the moral level, and then can be fought in negotiations from a position of moral strength, given that militarily and economically we will always be weaker than Israel and its supporters....*

*"I have always refused the premise that what we demand as a people
ought to be conceded to us charitably, or in bits and pieces as a reward
for our good behavior. This is to diminish ourselves and what we stand
for, since our position as a dispossessed people is morally unassailable."*
Palestinians are faced with a daunting task, not only of reclaiming
their narrative, their history, and their national cause, but of preserv-
ing and protecting their very presence on the lands of their birth.

In these final paragraphs, I can only provide the basic contours of a
vision and strategy for the future. I am acutely aware that I do not live
in the West Bank or Gaza Strip, and I do not face the daily grind of life
there under the combined grip of Israel and the Palestine Authority.
Yet, as a Palestinian, I can never shake off or escape my own skin, and,
therefore, I share with others a stake in the process and in the outcome. I am under no illusions about the enormity of the task ahead,
and about the array of forces mounted against us. The imbalance of
power between Israel and the Palestinians is not restricted to Israel's
military and technological superiority. Israel's ideological power, aided
and abetted by the U.S., which has enabled Israel to impose its version
of history and reality over the last half century, is perhaps even more
intimidating and overwhelming. So too is the fact that the PLO under
Arafat has largely submitted and succumbed to the power of this narrative, by lending its signature to the legitimization of this narrative
— committing, in effect, national suicide.

As I noted earlier, Palestinians have not disappeared, and now find
themselves, together with Jews, in the lands of historic Palestine. The
very structures that had been bent on destroying them have now to
accommodate Palestinians in some fashion. While it may appear that
these structures are fixed and unsurmountable, within these very structures there remains room for a new vision, for the power of truth, and
for the power of "no." This was accomplished during the intifada, and
can be so again. But it requires vision, strategy, and an evaluation of
methods and tactics consistent and congruent with the above.

Vision

*"I am not saying that we should advocate the destruction of Israel, nor
the dispossession of Israelis. Our movement gains its moral stature by*

its humane dimensions, its sincere willingness for coexistence, its firm belief in respecting the rights of others. What I am talking about is a new peace initiative designed over a long period of time to bring parity between us and the Israelis, who so far overpower us now as to make the moral dimension our only field of struggle. We must show Israel and its supporters that only a full acknowledgment by them of what was done to us can bring peace and reconciliation."

Cynics will retort that this vision is impossible, and detractors will find a million reasons why it is unachievable. But the value of a vision is not necessarily measured by immediate actions and reactions on the ground. The vision, in this case, is a bold statement that cuts through the rhetoric and holds up a mirror to Palestinians, Israelis, and the international community alike. Can people accept for themselves what they accept for others? Can people accept for others what they (refuse to) accept for themselves? In Israel/Palestine, a vision for the future rests on parity, on equality, on justice, on living in peace, security, and dignity in this shared homeland common to Palestinian-Arabs and Jewish-Israelis. It challenges both peoples to create the conditions of statehood commensurate with such a vision. It holds up a mirror to Israel (and by extension, to the U.S.) to show that there is a more moral, humane, and peaceful way to live on this land that is destined to contain both peoples for a long time to come. It offers a sense of possibilities that are not presently on the table, and a conviction that there is another way. Did the full force of the brutal apartheid era in South Africa deter the anti-apartheid movement? Did Nelson Mandela, as leader of the African National Congress (ANC), ever once confess defeat throughout the 27 years of his imprisonment? Did he once renounce the moral legitimacy of the anti-apartheid struggle? Did Blacks buckle under the weight of slavery and hundreds of years of oppression and dehumanization in the U.S. to give up their struggle for basic civil rights and equality? Why is it only on the Palestinian/Israeli front that similar efforts are deemed impossible?

The answer is perhaps two-fold. One, because so far, the Israeli-Zionist discourse has triumphed and prevailed. Israel has succeeded in portraying itself as a beacon of democracy and peace in the region instead of being shown up for what it is: as the "state of the Jewish people," Israel has institutionalized racism against others, particularly against the indigenous Palestinian inhabitants of that land. In this narrative, the history of forcibly robbing Palestinians of their homeland has been systematically attacked, deflected, and denied. The original sin against Palestinians has yet to be disseminated internationally in all its detail, immorality, and shame. Second, by signing the DOP and other accords, Palestinians have themselves harmed their cause by putting their stamp of approval on deals that in their very terms of reference and in every provision, contain renunciations of Palestinian legitimacy. In so doing,

Palestinians (the PLO) abdicated the higher moral ground of possessing an irrefutable case and cause, and capitulated to Israeli definitions that acknowledged no historical wrong, but would, for the sake of peace, offer some concessions to Palestinians living under its control.

Those of us who are troubled by these developments and are looking ahead into the future do not necessarily feel bound by Oslo or its provisions, which in any event did not invite our input nor acknowledge any aspect of the Palestinian national cause beyond the West Bank and Gaza Strip; vague references to "refugees" as an issue for "final status" negotiations notwithstanding.

While the PLO had in the past represented the Palestinian cause in its totality, the PA does not. Those of us outside the territories and omitted in the provisions of the "peace process" do not need to be intimidated or timid about renouncing the same frame of reference that has renounced our legitimate cause. We can have a role to play — alongside concerned others, Jewish, Israeli, American alike — in formulating and realizing that vision of a shared future.

Strategy

The strategy is simply this: to defeat Israel's political will. We have already noted the unequal power, and the fact that Palestinians cannot mobilize the military force required to overturn Israel's occupation and continued domination. Hence, they cannot defend or retake territory as such. The power they do possess is that of truth, of being there, of having legitimate rights that have not been realized. In defeating Israel's political will, Palestinians and their supporters have a fourfold task: (a) to defeat Israel's ability to rewrite history as though the original dispossession of Palestinians from Palestine was not as total as it was or was somehow justified by "war" or other events; (b) to defeat Israel's ability to impose a fait accompli on the territories today; (c) to deter Israel from achieving its vision of a permanent future settlement that marginalizes Palestinians in their own country; and (d) to defeat Israel in its attempt to erase Palestine altogether from the historical record.

At every level of countering Israel's political will to impose its version of reality over past, present, or future, Palestinians must challenge and defeat the regressive and outdated notion that somehow it is "right" for a state in the world today to exist exclusively of and for a single religio-ethnic group, especially when other religio-ethnic groups are indigenous to that same homeland — as are Christian and Muslim Palestinians.

Let us be clear about this: few Palestinians today, even fewer Israeli Jews, would willingly choose a binational state at this juncture.

Palestinians inside the West Bank and Gaza Strip who have suffered under immediate Israeli occupation would likely prefer separation, and a chance to exercise full sovereign national independence. So too would Palestinians exiled from or living outside of their homeland, who may never return, but long to know that a Palestinian national identity does exist, that they can claim it, possess its passport, and hold their heads high like any other legitimate nation in the world. Likewise, Palestinian refugees outside have always wanted to "go home" and have not abandoned their memories of their houses, villages, or lands. But these people have not seen Palestine for 50 years; their homes may no longer exist, and in any case, the reality is that Jewish Israelis have replaced them. There is no "going home" for Palestinians expelled in 1948 in this sense, but we need to make sure the same fate does not befall what is left of Palestine.

Until recently, Israeli Jews for the most part have never accepted the idea of two states, particularly if this involved relinquishing the territories occupied in 1967, especially East Jerusalem, and if it involved dismantling the hundreds of Jewish settlements established in these areas since then. While rejecting the notion of two states, most Israeli Jews would not want to contemplate a binational state, not with those people whom they have been taught to revile and hate and whom they associate with terror and fear. As for the Palestinians of Israel, their reactions have been mixed. Theoretically, since they already live in a de facto binational state, creating it officially would transform their status in Israel from that of a second- or third-class "minority," into one of full equality with Jews.

Officially, the Israeli government has advocated several solutions over the years, depending on circumstances and/or which political party was in power. These proposals have ranged from limited "self-rule" for Palestinians, confederation of parts of the West Bank with Jordan, withdrawal from Gaza, and since the DOP, the idea of setting up some kind of Palestinian entity or entities, a "satellite" state, that would keep major Israeli settlements intact, and involve very limited transfer of land and authority to the Palestinians. In this scenario, the Jordan River would remain Israel's "security border," East Jerusalem would remain part of Israel's "united and eternal capital," and major water resources in these areas would remain under Israeli control. Palestinian "independence" would be exercised and enjoyed *within* Israel.

Now a two-state solution has become physically and geographically improbable, given the placement of Jewish settlements across the "Green Line," and the myriad of roads that cut vertically and horizontally into the occupied areas. Two states have become politically passé — what is being created on the ground is a system of Palestinian Bantustans.

Methods

A viable strategy requires Palestinians to become proactive, as they did in the intifada, to take matters into their own hands and travel the long road to a future that is both free and fair. This begins with a concerted strategy to defeat Israel's political will and to offer instead their own vision of a peaceful future coexistence. In order to realize such a strategy that would deny and defeat Israel's ability to impose its own political solution on the Palestinians, and in order to approach this vision of a future that includes justice and equality for all, Palestinians must devise methods consistent with these imperatives.

In the years since the signing of the DOP, there has been evidence of innovative thinking among Palestinians, concerned Israelis, and Americans — Jews and others. Most have concurred on the point that Oslo "is dead," and something new must replace it before Israel succeeds in cementing a permanent solution that falls short of addressing the Palestinian issue in all its dimensions. As mentioned earlier, none of the Oslo documents recognize the applicability of international law beyond UN Security Council Resolutions 242 and 338 (UNSC 242 resolution does not refer to the Palestinians by name, it simply calls for addressing the problem of "refugees"). Even references to UN General Assembly Resolution 181 are absent. There is nothing, therefore, in these agreements that establishes a legal foundation — let alone indicate an intention — for a settlement based on two states. At best "Oslo" offers Palestinians "statelets." In response, many have reached the conclusion that the only remaining solution would have to be based on some form of binationalism for Jews and Arabs in all of Israel/Palestine.

For some, binationalism has been loosely defined as an arrangement whereby the two peoples would coexist in the geographical area of Palestine/Israel, with the details of political arrangements and government administration to be worked out at a later stage. For others, binationalism is necessarily predicated on the idea of a democratic and secular state. For this to be achieved, Israel, as the exclusive "state of the Jewish people," would have to be dismantled, and be replaced by Israel/Palestine as a state for its Jewish and Arab citizens alike, with full equality and rights for all.

Some of the new thinking has also centered around involving the Arab peoples in their respective countries in a process of reevaluating and resisting "normalization" of relations between Israel and various Arab and North African countries, until real progress has been made on arriving at a just solution to the Israeli/Palestinian conflict.

Unlike the intifada, where the strategic goal was to cause Israel's excessive power to backfire against itself, the goal at this juncture is more generally to expose goals and intentions behind Israeli rhetoric and ideology, and so neutralize and defeat Israel's customary sources of strength and power, and hence, its political will. In designing their methods of resistance, therefore, Palestinians would be organizing and mobilizing their strengths around their loci of power both inside and outside the occupied areas. Drawing on whatever established or newly-created organizational frameworks and resistance efforts they have at their disposal, Palestinians need to concentrate on introducing a compelling new discourse, one that is at once more difficult to counter and dismiss, and is more humane, just, and reasonable, than any solution currently offered. In order for that vision to be compelling and their strategy to succeed, Palestinians must pinpoint both their own strengths and weaknesses, undertake the same evaluation for Israel, and organize their methods and techniques of action accordingly.

We can summarize several areas where Palestinians can organize their resources and direct their energies toward defeating Israel's political will:

(a) At the level of the UN and other international organizations: Palestinians and their supporters can launch campaigns to alert the international community about ongoing human rights violations, and how the "peace process" has subverted and violated international law and UN resolutions concerning Palestine and the Palestinians.

(b) At the level of other Arab states and Arab peoples: To develop strategies of combating and resisting premature "normalization" with Israel.

(c) At the level of both the U.S. public and the public in Israel and elsewhere: To counter Israeli Zionist hegemony over the discourse, and to attract allies in the struggle for real equality and a just peace in a shared homeland.

(d) At the level of potentially friendly countries or groups: To exert direct economic or political leverage against Israel, or to work with the U.S. for it in turn to pressure Israel.

(e) At the level of the Palestinian diaspora: To insure the existence and visibility of a Palestinian national cause beyond the borders of Israel and the occupied areas, and to insure the viability of a (re)constituted organizational framework (in the form of the PLO or otherwise) to represent the Palestinian cause as a whole.

(f) At the level of the Palestinian community within the occupied areas: To check the excesses of power, corruption, and abuse by their own Authority, to contain and prevent extremist groups from engaging in terror attacks against Israeli civilians, and to mobilize and strengthen their own democratic and grassroots institutions and organizations, so as to lay foundations for a peaceful, law-abiding society that can reassure others about possibilities for a shared future.

This is a tall order, and at first glance, unrealistic and fanciful. But in reality, Palestinians are left with perhaps one final opportunity before the Israeli Zionist version of history forever prevails and replaces theirs.

What Palestinians have always had going for them is the force of truth, and the reality of their dispossession. But Palestinians have often damaged rather than served their cause, by engaging in terror and violence, and by lacking a coherent strategy. With the DOP, the very significant gains made by the intifada had been squandered. Palestinians submitted into signing a document that attested to their own defeat.

As the countdown to a resolution begins, it is time to remove the veiled fist that has hidden the sky for so long, and reach for the best the future can offer to these two peoples destined to share that troubled homeland. It is time to think, and work toward, the "unthinkable."

Sources

The bibliographic resources for this book are many. With reference to Deir Yassin the following books have been consulted and/or quoted from: Conor Cruise O'Brien, *The Siege: The Saga of Israel and Zionism* (New York: Simon and Schuster, 1986); Benjamin Beit-Hallahmi, *Original Sins: Reflections on the History of Zionism and Israel* (New York: Olive Branch Press, 1993); Benny Morris, *The Birth of the Palestinian Refugee Crisis, 1947-1949* (Cambridge: Cambridge University Press, 1987); Michael Palumbo, *The Palestinian Catastrophe: The 1948 Expulsion of a People from Their Homeland* (London: Quartet Books, 1987); Tom Segev, *1949: The First Israelis* (New York: Free Press, 1986); Yigal Allon, *Shield of David* (New York: Random House, 1970); Charles Smith, *Palestine and the Arab-Israeli Conflict*, 2nd edition (New York: St. Martin's Press, 1992); David Shipler, *Arab and Jew: Wounded Spirits in a Divided Land* (New York: Penguin, 1987); Sami Hadawi, *Bitter Harvest: A Modern History of Palestine* (New York: Olive Branch Press, 1991); J. Boyer Bell, *Terror Out of Zion: Irgun, Zvai Leumi, Lehi, and the Palestine Underground, 1929-1949* (New York: St. Martin's Press, 1977); Basheer K. Nijim, *Toward the De-Arabization of Palestine/Israel, 1945-1977* (Dubuque: Kendall/Hunt, 1984).

With reference to the history and contemporary situation of Israel/Palestine: Norman Finkelstein, *Image and Reality in the Israeli-Palestinian Conflict* (London: Routledge, 1995); Peter Grose, *Israel in the Mind of America* (New York: Knopf, 1983); Janet Abu-Lughod, "The Demographic War for Palestine," *The Link*, December 19, 1986; Ibrahim Abu-Lughod, ed., *The Transformation of Palestine*, (Evanston: Northwestern University Press, 1971); Raja Shehadeh, *Occupier's Law: Israel and the West Bank* (Washington, D.C.: Institute for Palestine Studies, 1985); Sara Roy, *The Gaza Strip: The Political Economy of Development* (Washington, D.C.: Institute of Palestine Studies, 1995); Edward W. Said, *The Question of Palestine* (New York, Vintage, 1979); Said, *Peace and Its Discontents: Essays on Palestine in the Middle East Process* (New York: Vintage, 1995).

For religious aspects relating to the questions facing Western Christians, Jews and Palestinian Christians and Muslims: Rosemary Radford Ruether and Herman J. Ruether, *The Wrath of Jonah: The Crisis of Religious Nationalism in the Israeli-Palestinan Conflict* (San Francisco: Harper & Row, 1989); Ian S. Lustick, *For the Land and the*

Lord: Jewish Fundamentalism in Israel (New York: Council on Foreign Relations, 1988); Rosemary Radford Ruether, *Faith and Fratricide: The Theological Roots of Anti-Semitism* (New York: Seabury Press, 1974); Naim Ateek, *Justice and Only Justice: A Palestinian Theology of Liberation* (Maryknoll: Orbis Press, 1989); Mitri Raheb, *I Am a Palestinian Christian* (Minneapolis: Fortress Press, 1995); Elias Chacour, *We Belong to the Land: The Story of a Palestinian Israeli Who Lives for Peace and Reconciliation* (San Francisco: Harper Collins, 1990); Paul Mendes-Flohr, ed., *A Land of Two Peoples: Martin Buber on Jews and Arabs* (Oxford: Oxford University Press, 1983); Israel Shahak, *Jewish History, Jewish Religion: The Weight of Three Thousand Years* (London: Pluto Press, 1994); Hannah Arendt, *Between Past and Future: Eight Exercises in Political Thought* (New York: Viking Press, 1961); Elie Wiesel, *A Jew Today* (New York: Vintage, 1978); Arthur Hertzberg, "An Open Letter to Elie Wiesel," New York Review of Books 35 (August 18, 1988); Marc H. Ellis, *Ending Auschwitz: The Future of Jewish and Christian Life* (Louisville: Westminster, 1994); Ellis, *Unholy Alliance: Religion and Atrocity in Our Time* (Minneapolis: Fortress, 1997), Ellis, *O Jerusalem: Embracing the Jewish Covenant in Our Time* (Minneapolis: Fortress, 1998); James Young, *The Texture of Memory: Holocaust Memorials and Meaning* (New Haven: Yale University Press, 1993); J. G. Davies, *Temples, Churches, and Mosques: A Guide to the Appreciation of Religious Architecture* (Oxford: Basil Blackwell, 1982); Carter Heyward, Anne Gilson, et al., *Revolutionary Forgiveness: Feminist Perspectives on Nicaragua* (Maryknoll: Orbis, 1987).

Contributors

Sheila Cassidy is an independent researcher on Middle East political, religious, and historical affairs. Her special areas of interest are Palestine and the Gulf. She currently heads Riverside Middle East Research Project, a consortium of independent researchers.

Souad Dajani is an American of Palestinian origin. She received her Ph.D. in sociology from the University of Toronto in 1984, and her M.A. and B.A. degrees from the American University of Beirut, Lebanon. She works in Massachusetts and teaches part-time at various colleges in the area. Her first book, *Eyes Without Country: Searching for a Palestinian Strategy of Liberation* was published in 1994 by Temple University Press.

Marc H. Ellis is a Jewish thinker who specializes in modern Judaism and post-Holocaust thought. His writings include *Toward a Jewish Theology of Liberation; Ending Auschwitz: The Future of Jewish and Christian Thought; Unholy Alliance: Religion and Atrocity in Our Time*; and *O Jerusalem: Embracing the Jewish Covenant in Our Time*. He has taught at the Maryknoll School of Theology and Florida State University as well as being a Senior Fellow and Visiting Scholar at Harvard University.

Muhammad Hallaj was born in Palestine and has had a distinguished career in education and public policy analysis both in Palestine and in the United States. He has been a visiting scholar at Harvard University's Center for International Affairs and for many years was the director of the Palestine Research and Educational Center in Washington, D.C. and editor of its magazine, *Palestine Perspectives*.

Salma Khadra Jayyusi is a Palestinian poet, critic, literary historian and anthologist. She is founder and director of East-West Nexus/PROTA in Boston and London and of Al-Manara in Jordan. After teaching at several Arab and American universities, she founded PROTA in 1980 for the translation of the best in Arabic literature. Over thirty volumes have been accomplished since, including five anthologies of Arabic literature. In 1995 she founded East-West Nexus to deal with ideas and discourse vis á vis the Arab world and the West. She is the author of *Trends and Movements in Modern Arabic Poetry* and the editor of *The Legacy of Muslim Spain*.

Rami G. Khoury is former editor-in-chief of the *Jordan Times*. He is a widely-read syndicated columnist and television commentator based in Amman, Jordan.

Daniel McGowan is the founder and current director of Deir Yassin Remembered, whose roots grew from seed planted by the Eyewitness Israel Program sponsored by the American-Arab Anti-Discrimination Committee (ADC) during the intifada. He is a professor of economics at Hobart and William Smith Colleges in Geneva, New York.

Fuad Bassim Nijim was born in Jerusalem and grew up on the West Bank under Israeli occupation. He studied studio arts, architecture, and economics at Saint Olaf College and the University of Minnesota. After working in city planning in the United States, he is completing graduate studies in Community and Regional Development at the University of California at Davis. Nijim is serving on the board of advisers of Deir Yassin Remembered.

Meir Pa'il, a retired Israeli colonel and military historian, was sent by the Haganah to observe and critique the attack on Deir Yassin; it was the first joint military operation by the Jewish terrorist gangs known as the Irgun Zwai Leumi (Irgun) and the Lehi (the Stern Gang). Pa'il's written account and photographs of the massacre are to this day sealed in the Israeli military archives.

Rosemary Radford Ruether is the Georgia Harkness Professor of Applied Theology at the Garrett Evangelical Seminary. She is the author of numerous books including *Faith and Fratricide: The Image of the Jews in Early Christianity* and *The Wrath of Jonah: The Crisis of Religious Nationalism in the Israeli-Palestinian Conflict*.

Pat McDonnell Twair is an award-winning journalist who has specialized in writing on the culture and politics of the Middle East for the past 20 years. Her articles appear regularly in the *Washington Report on Middle East Affairs*, *The Middle East* and *Aramco World*. She is completing a book on the six years she spent in Syria, under the title *Ma'alish*.

Bibliography

Arui, Naseer, *The Obstruction of Peace: The U.S., Israel and the Palestinians,* Monroe, ME: Common Courage Press, 1996.

Asali, K.J., *Jerusalem in History,* Northampton, MA: Olive Branch Press/Interlink, 1990.

Beit-Hallahmi, Bejamin, *Original Sins: Reflections on the History of Zionism and Israel,* Northampton, MA: Olive Branch Press/Interlink, 1993.

Bennis, Phyllis & Moushabeck, Michel (eds.), *Beyond the Storm: A Gulf Crisis Reader,* Northampton, MA: Olive Branch Press/Interlink, 1991.

Chomsky, Noam, *The Fateful Triangle: The United States, Israel and the Palestinians,* Boston: South End Press, 1993.

Fisk, Robert, *Pity the Nation: The Abduction of Lebanon,* New York: Atheneum, 1990.

Flapan, Simha, *The Birth of Israel: Myths and Realities,* New York: Pantheon, 1987.

Giannou, Chris, *Beseiged: A Doctor's Story of Life and Death in Beirut,* Northampton, MA: Olive BranchPress/Interlink, 1992.

Gowers, Andrew & Walker,Tony, *Behind the Myth: Yasser Arafat and the Palestinian Revolution,* New York: Olive Branch Press/Interlink, 1991.

Hourani, Albert, *A History of the Arab Peoples,* Cambridge, MA: Harvard University Press, 1991.

Lockman, Zachary & Beinin, Joel (eds.), *Intifada: The Palestinian Uprising Against Israeli Occupation,* Boston: South End Press, 1989.

Lynd, Staughton, Bahour, Sam & Lynd, Alice, *Homeland: Oral Histories of Palestine and Palestinians,* Northampton, MA: Olive Branch Press/Interlink, 1994.

McDowall, David, *Palestine and Israel: The Uprising and Beyond,* Los Angeles & Berkeley: University of California Press, 1989.

Rodinson, Maxime, *Cult, Ghetto and State: The Persistence of the Jewish Question,* New York & London: Saqi Books, 1983.

Sabbagh, Suha (ed.), *Arab Women: Between Defiance and Restraint,* Northampton, MA: Olive Branch Press/Interlink, 1996.

Said, Edward W. & Hitchens, Christopher (eds.), *Blaming the Victims: Spurious Scholarship and the Palestinian Question,* London & New York: Verso, 1988.

Said, Edward W., *Covering Islam: How the Media and the Experts Determine How We See the Rest of the World,* New York: Pantheon, 1981.

Said, Edward W., *Peace and Its Discontents,* New York: Vintage, 1996.

Said, Edward W., *The Question of Palestine,* New York: Times Books, 1979.

Shipler, David K., *Arab and Jew: Wounded Spirits in a Promised Land,* New York: Times Books, 1986.